Wannabe WARRIOR

BREAKING FREE OF THE DIRTY
LITTLE LIES THAT KEEP US SMALL

KELLY CLEEVE

Published and distributed by Merack Publishing.

Cleeve, Kelly, 1979 -

Wannabe Warrior: Breaking Free of the Dirty, Little Lies That Keep Us Small

ISBN 978-1-949635-68-3

Cover and Interior by Yvonne Parks at PearCreative.ca

DEDICATION

Para Miguel, quien tomó de mi mano, mientras
limpiaba mi nariz y mis lágrimas cuando tenía miedo.
Tienes mi corazón.

For Miguel, who held my hand and wiped my tears
(and my nose) when I was afraid.
You have my heart.

CONTENTS

Prologue: Warrior, Who?   1

Introduction: The Mentorship   7

Chapter 1
Their Lives are Better Than Mine   23

Chapter 2
The Bright Side is the Only Side   37

Chapter 3
Love Should Be Easy   67

Chapter 4
This is Not What a Family Looks Like   89

Chapter 5
You are a Terrible Parent   111

Chapter 6
You are Not Worthy   127

Chapter 7
You ARE Depression   141

Chapter 8
The Only Way to Walk Past Fear is to Walk Through It   161

Conclusion   168

Epilogue   177

Acknowledgments   179

About the Author   183

Prologue
WARRIOR, WHO?

Years ago, someone told me my name means "warrior woman". I recently looked it up, and lo and behold, it's true.

Kelly ~ comes from the Gaelic tradition, and means warrior. It is a very popular Irish name, also associated with war, liveliness and aggression.

I have so many thoughts about this. I don't even know where to start.

When I first caught a glimpse of the meaning behind my name, I thought, *Well, that doesn't fit.* Warriors are strong and fierce. They are the personification of bravery. I'm not brave. I'm a scaredy girl, laden with worries, always doing the right thing, the *safe* thing. I'm brave when I have to be, when there appears to be no other choice. And even then, my first thought is usually, *Shit!*

I wish I felt like the warrior who stares fear in the face, hair blowing in the wind (in a sexy way, and in the right direction so my luscious locks don't get stuck in my lip gloss). I would stand tall, put my hands on my hips, stick my boobs out, and bellow, *How dare you try and stop me!*

Nope. I am the girl who overthinks every decision, second guesses my instincts, and cries when I know the right answer is not the one I want to face. I feel the fear. It's a grip on my heart, a roadblock in my mind, a tingle at the base of my neck, a heavy pit in my stomach. The fear is always with me, a shadow of *what if…* Despite this momentary hesitation, I force myself to squeeze my eyes shut, cross my fingers and step into the abyss of the great unknown.

It seems ironic that my name is associated with the word "aggression". Nope, that's not me. They've got the wrong girl. I was raised to be a good girl. The girl who makes practical choices, who puts others above herself, who has perfected the art of polite manners. I am the girl who smiles—even when my insides are a swirling storm of rage or self-deprecation. I associate the word "aggressive" with the words "cocky" and worse, "bitchy". I am *not* aggressive. I am likeable, loyal and dependable. Aggression turns people off. Ew.

Now, "war", I can get behind. This feels more like me. War is an old college sweater. It's torn, stained and ugly as hell—but it feels familiar. I know its texture, its smell. It's a tattered piece of clothing I would never wear out in public but I just can't bring myself to throw away. I don't even like it, really, but it's become a piece of me, a part of my story.

For as long as I can remember, I have been at war with myself. I have been an unwitting player in an epic battle between the person I am expected to be, the person I want to be, and the person I feel I really am. This battle began in my childhood, before I was self-aware enough to know I was at war. As the firstborn child in my family, I fulfilled all the expected roles: good student, well-behaved child, responsible big sister, and loving daughter. There was no room to experiment with who *I* wanted to be because I was so busy pleasing everyone else. Each admiring smile, each compliment, each pat on the head kept The Warrior within me quiet and subdued. In fact, I didn't know I was at war until adulthood, when this good-girl mentality caused me to marry the wrong man. I had walked sleepily through my life, without questioning expectations, and when I finally woke up, I found myself standing in the middle of a battlefield.

I was a beautiful bride, draped in white, hair pulled back to reveal youthful, glowing skin. I stood tall in my stilettos, smiled graciously, blushed with bashful innocence and greeted my guests with gratitude. I made a lovely speech, danced with my father and with my new husband. I remembered not to drink too much champagne and to check my hair and makeup once in a while. I did and said all the things a young woman is supposed to the moment before she steps into her future.

The Warrior slept.

I was a charming young wife. I took pride in cleaning my house and raising my two adorable babies. I went to work, had coffee with girlfriends, walked the dog, made supper for my family and exercised at the gym. I knew the neighbors by name and invited them over for cocktails. I hosted dinner parties, children's birthday parties, baby showers, bachelorette evenings, girls' nights and family get-togethers. I did and said all the things a young woman is supposed to when she is becoming a responsible adult.

The Warrior was stirring.

A few years after the wedding, The Warrior sat up, stretched her aching body after a long slumber, rubbed the sleep out of her eyes and looked around. "Who have you become?" she wondered.

The truth is, the woman I was trying to be on the outside did not match the woman I was inside. The woman I masqueraded as was calm and content. She was simple and serene. She was a doting mother, a caring wife, an inspiring teacher. She appreciated her peaceful, predictable life, living in a beautiful house, on a quiet, tree-lined street. She was grateful for her blessings and felt that wanting more was a betrayal of all she had been given. In quiet moments though, this woman felt the life she had created didn't fit. It was confining. A soft, persistent whisper told the woman she was meant for more, that she should be chasing something bigger. The whisper told the woman it was okay to want more, to *be* more. It reassured her it was not only acceptable to chase her dreams, but that she deserved to.

The woman I was trying to be was small. She colored inside the lines and carefully stayed in her lane, never straying, or doing the unexpected. She never chased excitement or risk. She was safe, but she was unhappy. There was another woman inside, bursting to claw her way out, to experience the world on a grander level. This woman was, indeed, a warrior.

The Warrior is fierce. She's a certified badass—powerful and confident. She declares that aggression is not necessarily negative. One can be aggressive in going after their dreams, in creating a life worth living. "Aggressive" can be associated with "ambitious". It's not cocky, it's courageous.

I realized The Warrior had been within me all along, hibernating, waiting. It just took 40 years for me to hear her. It was a shocking, ground-shaking revelation. Once I knew she was there, I couldn't *unknow*. The Warrior challenged me to examine my life and the woman I had become.

"Why aren't you living your best life?" she demanded. "What is holding you back?"

All instincts instructed me to listen carefully to every word The Warrior had to say. She is a truth-teller and telling the truth is a brave and defiant act in and of itself. The truth calls for aggressive action, for change, and for growth. It isn't always pretty and is—more often than not—terrifying. I knew the journey The Warrior would lead me on would be painful, confusing and, at times, shameful. I would fall. I would become lost. I would be bloodied. I would cry. I would be alone. I would call out for mercy, yet I wanted to walk *toward* The Warrior—not away from her. Despite the magnitude of the challenge she placed before me—to live my best life and become a new woman—I innately understood I was ready to rise to the occasion.

In knowing The Warrior, I could never remain the same version of myself.

"Where have you been all my life?" I asked The Warrior, somewhat resentful I had gone so many years and made so many mistakes without knowing her.

"I was caged," she replied.

"Caged by what?"

She answered without hesitation. "I was caged by fear. When I awoke, I looked around and saw the life you had created and I felt your discontent. Your unhappiness was quiet, though, forbidden. It was silenced by your fear. You weren't ready to meet me yet, so I stayed behind the iron bars of judgment, shame and guilt."

"I want you to be free," I declared.

"I want *you* to be free," she echoed.

As I have come to know The Warrior within me, I have learned I can rely on her to carry me through challenging times. She's like a superhero cape I put on when I feel afraid or anxious, when I know I need to make the difficult choice. She's the one who urges me to put my big-girl panties on, because we are going to take over the world. The Warrior is the woman I want to be. I have moments when I pretend to be her, and even fleeting moments when I *am* her, however, she and I are not synonymous. Yet.

It seems, in my name, there lies a predetermined destiny, though I'm not sure I believe in such a thing. Maybe I *am* a warrior woman. I am no longer willing to lie down and be safe. That feels like playing dead—and I am alive, burning with ambition, with the incessant need to grow. Maybe I *am* a fighter, the one who will stare fear in the face after all—though not with grace and fearlessness, but with trembling knees and a knowing in my heart. Did my mother understand all of this when she named me? Did she have an inkling I was made for more?

Over time, I have learned it was fear that held me back from living the life I knew I was meant for. Fear whispered in my ears and told stories of failure, judgment and tragedy. Fear kept me small.

I am done with being small. I'm over it! The more I see fear in my life, the more I know I need to face it in order to break free of the chains which hold me down. It's another war, perhaps, but one I feel I am in control of because I hold the battle plans within my hands. Each time I face fear, I win the battle. If I continue to rise up against the urge to stay small and safe, I will eventually win the war—thereby changing my own course in history. Eventually, I won't be pretending to be brave. I will *become* brave. I will *become* fierce and aggressive. I will *become* The Warrior.

I'm not there yet. My first instinct is not to fight fear, but to flee. I still find myself saying, *This is scary. This is hard. This is risky. This is uncertain.* The difference is, now there is a voice which comes in behind all of this fear and asks, *Yes, but can you do it anyway?* I may not *be* The Warrior, but I am content to be

The Warrior's apprentice: examining, questioning, pondering, practicing, and learning.

I am a Wannabe Warrior. For now.

Introduction
THE MENTORSHIP

The Warrior is teaching me about fear. "Look around you," she says. "It's everywhere."

"I don't see it," I respond, "people seem happy."

"Fear," she explains, "is like the famous line at the end of the movie, "The Usual Suspects": The greatest trick the Devil ever pulled was convincing the world he didn't exist."

"Fear is so quiet, we often forget he's there, but don't be fooled. He's a deceptive little bastard. Fear is quiet, but not meek. It is a powerful emotion which can seep into every aspect of your life, casting shade over your experiences, your reactions and your relationships. It whispers to you so faintly you may not hear it. And if you do, it has tricked you into believing it is your own voice and the words you hear in your head are the truth. *You are not enough. You are not loved. You are a fraud.* Fear laughs as it manipulates and controls our actions like an expert puppeteer. *Don't go into the unknown. Stay here, where it's safe. Don't put yourself out there. Keep your true self close and protected. Don't reach out to others. They are not like you. They are different. Judgmental. Better. Danger! Danger! Danger!*"

"Don't believe him. Don't let him hold power over you. Don't let him keep you small. Don't let him beat you. Stand strong and rise above Fear. Become the woman you want to be, despite Fear."

"I'm listening, Warrior," I say, with bated breath, "tell me more."

> Too many of us are not living our dreams because we are living our fears.
> Les Brown

Let me begin by sharing. At one point or another, I believed all the dirty, little lies that serve as chapter titles in this book. I still struggle with many of them. You might assume, because I am writing this book, I have dug deep and found bravery— that I stared fear in the face and told it to take a hike. That's not the case. As it turns out, I am a big, fat chicken! The list of fears I carry in my back pocket is longer than my grocery list. What qualifies me to write this book is the fact I am aware of my fears, and wish to expose their power in an effort to loosen their white-knuckled grip on my life. I no longer wish to be controlled or manipulated. I want to be free from the limitations fear places upon me.

I have a tattoo on the inside of my left wrist, which reads *fearless*. The word was permanently imprinted on my skin two weeks after filing for divorce—a time in my life when fear was my predominant emotion. I was well aware of its power, of the way it held me down and made me small in a marriage which was unfulfilling, and how it left me numb to the life I had created. I knew it was time to take off the shackles before the numbness became my life sentence. The future—post-divorce—which lay ahead of me, felt vast, unknown and terrifying. I had made the scariest decision of my life and was about to fully immerse myself in the consequences of it. I needed to find the courage to face the reality of my rocky financial situation. I needed to allow the judgment of my friends and family to wash over me, and find strength in knowing I made the right choice. I needed to muster up the bravery to stare my cherub-faced children in the eyes and feel every ounce of their heartbreak. I needed to find a new sense of self, to define this woman I had become. That period of my life was petrifying.

The tattoo is certainly not a celebration of my bravery. The tattoo is not even an aspiration of who, or what, I long to be. I don't want to be fearless. That's an impossible and ridiculous aspiration. In the brilliant words of Patricia Knight, "There can be no bravery without fear." I think it's natural to be afraid—sometimes. People who claim they have no fear are either a) robot aliens from outer space, b) in denial and out of touch with their emotions, or c) completely full of shit. The tattoo serves as a reminder to evaluate the validity of my fears and is a stamp of encouragement, reminding me to lean into discomfort. I never want to make decisions based in fear. I don't want fear to hold me back from what is right, what is true or what is meant for me. Decisions based in fear tend to narrow your world, and restrict your life experiences. I want to rise above my fear, let my intuition be my guide and *go for it*.

Every single time I have faced my fear, I have been better off for it. I may not do it with fierceness or with grace, but I have always been proud of the decisions I've made. I *want* to tell you it gets easier with experience, but it doesn't. It's difficult. Every. Single. Time. But, here's what I *can* tell you ...

Fear would have kept me in a loveless marriage with my first husband. Fear would have locked my children in my home, protecting them from the dangers of the outside world. Fear would never have let me earn a Master's Degree or venture into a new career, following my life's true passions. Fear would have deleted the dating apps and eliminated the opportunity to find true love. Fear would have taken my mental health and left me in a world of gray hopelessness. Fear would have left my second marriage in ruins.

Let's play a game for a moment. Close your eyes and imagine your life free of, and unencumbered by, fear. What would you do if you weren't afraid? What would you try? Bungee jumping? Eating dinner in a restaurant, alone? Approaching the gorgeous girl or sultry guy you see every morning in the coffee shop? Applying for the promotion you know you deserve?

What would it *feel* like to have no fear? Powerful? Calming? Exhilarating?

Yes, I know fear is healthy. It protects us from dangerous situations, causing the little hairs on the back of our necks to tingle. It creates a foreboding nausea which motivates us to study for an exam or to prepare for an important presentation. It keeps us healthy by reminding us to avoid fatty foods and chemical-laden products. It holds a worry about our planet's fate and encourages us to reduce our carbon footprint. Yes, some level of fear is good—necessary even. But what happens when fear becomes the predominant emotion in our daily lives? What is the quality of our lives when fear trumps joy, ease, and relaxation?

No one would intentionally choose a life based in fear. Why would you? It feels heavy. Paralyzing. In fact, we are trained from a very early age to ignore fear and focus on happiness. For countless generations, parents have read fairy tale stories with happy endings. We watch movies where, after some tribulation, the boy gets the girl and they live happily ever after. We listen to love songs and wonder when we will meet the one who makes our heart flutter. We are inundated with memes about happiness that plaster the walls of our social media. We buy our children t-shirts which have the word "Happiness" printed across a glittering sequined rainbow. Happiness is everywhere we look. It's a bright and shiny expectation, available to all of us who are good, kind and deserving. However, what happens when we grow up and find happiness is not necessarily easy to achieve? How does that affect our self-concept and self-esteem?

Most of us spend our adult lives obsessively chasing happiness. We search the world for our soulmate, scouting friend groups and online forums for that perfect match who will be the cherry atop the ice cream sundae of life. We organize evenings with our friends, laughing and drinking wine in the flattering glow of candle light, so we may feel moments of belonging. We attend yoga classes, meditation groups and personal growth seminars to find our inner peace. We buy the next best iPhone, car, or lipstick—fulfilling our need for instant gratification. We spend copious hours at the gym, or buy the newest anti-wrinkle face cream, or consult plastic surgeons. We line up outside the therapist's office. Maybe he has the answer to unlock the elusive secret which will bring life's happiness …

I sound cynical. I know it. The truth is, I have always struggled with the term "happiness" and with the pressure society places on us to find it. For those of us who aren't jumping on the couch with happiness overflowing from our every orifice, fear tells us we mustn't be good enough, kind enough, or deserving enough. I don't know about you, but for me, happiness has not always been easy to find. It comes in small waves, tiny moments when life feels just right, and then it slips away again—and I am left feeling cold and confused. Is there something wrong with me? Why do I feel as if I am standing in the darkness, watching everyone around me experience a life of joy and ease? Don't I deserve to live that life too?

Despite the outward appearance of ease and joy, I think everyone around me is on a lifelong pilgrimage to find happiness. We search all around us, with varying levels of desperation. We look to our partners. We look to find fulfillment in raising our children. We look to find meaning in our jobs. We crave gratification in material items and retail therapy. We long for peace and try to find it in actual therapy. Unknowingly, subconsciously, we are all combating fear—worried we may never find the secret to happiness and trying to convince ourselves we deserve it. The irony is, we don't even know it's fear driving our obsessive search for joy. And, on top of that, we are searching in all the wrong places. What if happiness can't be found outside of us at all? What if the attainment of happiness can only come from within us? What if the only way to find joy is to exorcise fear?

I tend to be a highly emotional person. My husband, Miguel, refers to it as "making waves." I feel my emotions in technicolor—they are loud and vibrant, coming and going quickly, like waves crashing on the sand. My reactions are instantaneous and often lack a filter. I lead with emotion, and logic quickly steps in to intervene when necessary, but is always a second place finisher in this race. In addition to this charming—and sometimes off-putting— trait I am also a chronic overthinker. It is my greatest strength and most-crippling weakness. The proverbial double-edged sword. Tediously considering emotions and situations is what allows me to be empathetic, and to see multiple perspectives of a problem. It also shackles the weight of anxiety to my ankle if I am not paying attention. Sometimes, my mind gets the best of me. I'll give you an example.

A few months ago, tragedy struck my community. A young boy (early in his adolescence and eager to fit in with an older crowd) decided to experiment with drugs while hanging out at a skateboard park. The older boys—amused by their younger schoolmate's unabashed desperation to be part of the group—used his vulnerability against him, encouraging him to take more and more of the deadly pills. As his body rejected the astronomical quantity of drugs he ingested, he began to panic in his delirium. The older boys found the situation to be … hilarious. Instead of using their cell phones to call for help, they videotaped the boy's delusional and erratic behavior, posting it on their social media for the amusement of their friends. In his dying moments, this young soul was stripped of dignity and humanity, his death a source of entertainment for his peers. Upon hearing the news, my town erupted in horrified shock and outrage.

The logical part of me recognizes not only the tragedy of the situation, but the inherent complexity of it. I am aware of powerful phenomena such as "groupthink" and "mob mentality". In truth, we all may be merely a moment away from succumbing to such pressure and making terrible mistakes. I wonder about the upbringing of the older boys, about the possibility they may carry their own traumas. I understand that stories portrayed in the media are not always as they seem, that the truth is sometimes buried, manipulated or altered to create sensational headlines. My logical brain, however, was not the one who felt the heaviness of this story. None of this logic mattered enough to soften the visceral reaction of a mother's heart.

My girlfriends and I discussed the event incessantly. Our children were roughly the same age as the boy who died, and the news shook our fragile sense of security. Our hearts broke for his parents. Our hearts palpitated for our own children who were beginning high school in mere weeks. We worried about what they would be exposed to, and we prayed they would be savvy enough to make responsible choices. After a day or two, the story was forgotten by most. But not by me. It hovered above me, like a dark cloud of impending doom.

This tragedy boggled my mind on so many levels and I couldn't let it go. As someone who speaks and writes about emotional development and has made a career of providing parenting advice, I was astounded by the lack of empathy displayed by the older boys. While my heart bled for the victim's family, I spent most of my time thinking about the families of the boys who videotaped this episode. What if my son stood by and watched another die? How does a parent react to *that*?

Most parents I know carry a healthy amount of fear in their back pocket at all times. It's a low-burning fire which reminds us to keep our children safe, to be mindful of our parenting practices. Thinking about these adolescent boys threw gasoline onto the fire and my fear exploded. *Am I doing a good enough job as a mother? Would my child be confident enough not to need the approval of others? Would he decline the offer of illicit substances? What would he do if he saw another child suffering? Would he stand up against those who were cold and cruel? Would he call for help, or succumb to peer pressure?*

After days of self-flagellation and uncertainty over the effectiveness of my parenting, my husband intervened. He reminded me I had invested thirteen years in raising a smart, responsible, and kind child. I intentionally cultivate meaningful dialogue with all of my children, and work hard to keep the lines of communication open. I invite honesty and tough conversations. No topic or question is off-limits in our family. I spend time building connection with them, strengthening our bond. I know their friends. I know how they spend their time on the internet, and I encourage them to keep a healthy balance in regard to tech time. My teenager—all my children—would be fine, Miguel said.

Then he asked a question, which we often use in complicated emotional times, "What story are you telling yourself right now?"

Instead of telling myself I could trust my parenting and trust my son, I had created a story that made the possibility of tragedy not miniscule, but *likely*. Fear had gotten the best of me and was whispering lies into my ear.

Being a relatively self-aware person, I can admit that parenting is the arena in which I frequently need to fight against fear. I began to wonder, though, what other stories I had been telling myself. What other areas of my life have been influenced by fear? Is this tendency isolated to my parenting, or does it seep into other areas of my life? After some soul-searching and honest introspection, I realized many aspects of my life are, in fact, colored by fear. I had become so comfortable with the emotion, it barely registered with me anymore. I am afraid of growing older, looking at the new wrinkles appearing on my face. I worry I'm not going to be financially prepared for retirement and will be unable to live the adventurous life I long for. I fear starting a new career and wonder if it's too late or too risky to make such a bold move. I think about the health of my parents and other loved ones who are aging. I lose sleep over my marriage, desperately craving peace within a complex relationship. Mostly, though, I worry about my children, about their well-being and about the complicated dynamics of raising a blended family. Yes, it seems fear snuck up and took over my life, like a ninja who takes you out before you can even scream.

Surely, I can't be the only human who feels this way. *Please, Lord, say it's not just me.*

I began to look outward at society, with this new and inquisitive lens. Like a sexy, sleuthy, female version of Sherlock Holmes, I observed my family, my friends and my colleagues. I investigated my social media feeds, the shows I watch and the news I am inundated with. And I saw fear everywhere. Fear of not fitting in. Fear of rejection. Fear of judgment. Fear of missing out. (That one even has its own trendy acronym, FOMO, which has become common jargon in our culture's vocabulary!) Fear seems to have permeated every aspect of our being, from family life, to work, to the social image we create. Oh my god, what is this doing to our mental health?! Do people *know* that fear has taken over their lives and their bodies?! Of course they don't know. If they did, wouldn't they be as shocked and appalled as I am? But … how could they *not* know?

In my research on human development and emotional intelligence, I have read many articles that state today's children have a resting heart rate which is substantially higher than the medical norm. In layman's terms, children no longer know what it feels like to be calm. Their body's natural "resting place" is in fight-or-flight mode. It makes complete sense! Too many children have schedules jam-packed with extracurricular activities. They are shuttled around from hockey practice to tutoring to birthday parties, to music lessons. Why? Because their parents are afraid of boredom. Afraid their children are missing out because all the other children get to experience these things. Afraid their kids won't be accepted into great colleges. Afraid too much free time will inevitably lead to trouble. And when the children come home, many of them are being raised by stressed out, disconnected parents. Parents who are working so hard to keep up an image they may not be able to afford. Parents who are exhausted and working long hours because they're afraid of missing the next mortgage payment.

If you are reading this thinking—*Damn! I'm glad I don't have kids!*—don't relax too much. I have a sneaking suspicion fear has gotten to you as well. Let's investigate, shall we? Are you afraid of being overlooked at work? Afraid of disappointing your parents? Afraid of missing out on a great song, a great party, a great adventure? Afraid you are not living up to your true potential? Afraid you're not following your dreams? Afraid you'll be single forever? Yes, fear has gotten to you too, hasn't it? I hate to say I told you so.

I wonder if our society is even aware of the amount of fear we carry around. My guess is we've become so accustomed to its weight, we no longer feel it. My goal in writing this book is to create an awareness of the running dialogue in our minds. I want to discern the voice of fear when I hear it, and know it does not speak the truth. I want to be mindful of the role fear plays in my decision-making, how it aims to keep me small instead of allowing me to grow. I want to see the effects it has on my life and my relationships. Awareness is the first step to making change. It's a tiny, but powerful, step away from fear, moving toward freedom. Toward joy.

When I was in the middle of writing this book, a worldwide health crisis broke out and the degree to which fear overtook logic was undeniable. A virus was rampant, making millions sick, killing thousands. As the virus began to touch all continents, the word "pandemic" was used and all hell broke loose. The world, essentially, lost its freaking mind. As someone who was immersed in research about fear, I found society's response fascinating and alarming—in equal parts. This book, it appeared, was hitting the nail right on the head. The undercurrent of fear I was pondering broke open like a geyser overnight.

The world has seen and survived epidemics before, even in my lifetime, yet I have never seen such irrational behavior on a global scale. I wondered what was different this time around. Then I came across the following statistic, and had an A-ha moment which shed light on our current fear mentality. Not surprisingly, the media had reported on previous viruses. In the heyday of their devastating reigns, Ebola received 11.1 million mentions in the news, HIV 40 million, and SARS had 56.2 million mentions. In the first few *weeks* of media coverage, COVID-19 Coronavirus received a staggering 1.1 billion nods in the news and that reached 2.1 billion in the months that followed. That's right, I said BILLION. And, not all the news is coming from respectable, reputable sources. When your next-door neighbor, Tom, posts a video on Facebook of grocery carts stacked high with canned goods, you begin to wonder if you should be lining up too. So the question becomes, why did we react this way? Fear.

For the first time in history, we are inundated with media to the degree where it's difficult to turn it off. Our overwhelmed prefrontal cortex needs an occasional break from the stress and chatter, but it's almost impossible to take a quiet moment to settle our thoughts and slow our heart rates because our phones are blowing up with constant notifications. Our obsessive need to check them has become our society's addiction. Thus, the media stokes the slow burning embers of fear.

This book tells the story of how fear has affected my life and the ongoing battle I fight to push back against it. This is the story of how I came to recognize my fears in an attempt to reclaim my freedom. Each chapter title shares a lie that Fear told me at one point or another. Perhaps you will recognize yourself in some of these lies and begin your journey toward love and liberty. Maybe you will see a loved one who is affected by these limitations and gain valuable insight to better support the people in your life.

It feels bold to say I hope to change the undertone of our society, but I suppose I am that obnoxious, ambitious girl. I hope one conversation will lead to another conversation, which will eventually lead to a societal conversation. Why are we letting our lives be controlled by fear? It's unintentional, I'm sure. We weren't even aware there *was* a problem. Until now.

Once you open your eyes to something, it's very hard to close them again. You can't unsee a new reality. So, now what? We can either shrug our shoulders and turn our cheeks, or we can face our fears head on and unpack some of the baggage we have been carrying.

Because I know it's not an easy conversation to have, I'll go first and break the ice. So, sit back, grab a glass of wine and read on as I expose my deepest, darkest fears. It won't hurt my feelings if you roll your eyes at the things that worry me. It's even okay if you laugh a little. In fact, I hope you do. Humor is an excellent way of disarming a difficult topic. However, I hope that despite the irrationality or ridiculousness of some of my fears, my vulnerability inspires you to investigate some of the stories you are telling yourself. Are you harboring any fears that hold you back from joy, from achieving your dreams, or from living your best life?

At the end of each chapter, you will find a journal page, providing a safe space for you to explore the stories and lies Fear may be telling you. I encourage you not to skip over this self-reflection. It's okay if you wish to simply enjoy the book and read about my struggles purely for entertainment's sake, but truthfully, I have higher hopes for you, my friend. Don't be *afraid* to do the work. (Do you see what I did there?)

I wrote this book to begin a dialogue which will free us from the restraints Fear places upon us. How can you have meaningful conversation if you don't know where you stand? Such introspection will certainly be uncomfortable, I'm not going to mislead you, but be strong, dear reader. Once you recognize your fears, the power they have to hold you down and make you small is diminished. You will sense your fears creeping up on you and coloring your reactions because you've pulled away the invisibility cloak they previously hid beneath. The journey we are about to embark on will be challenging, yes, but it will be worth it. I promise.

Imagine living a life free of fear.

Imagine breaking free of the hold fear places upon you.

Imagine ripping off the chains, which keep you small and restrict you from taking up the space you deserve.

Imagine becoming your own warrior.

Imagine the possibilities ...

Chapter 1

FEAR SAYS:
"THEIR LIVES ARE
BETTER THAN MINE"

I love social media as much as the next girl. You can often find me sipping my morning coffee, scrolling through my Facebook and Instagram feeds. *Often?* Liar, liar, pants on fire! It happens Every. Single. Morning. I love the motivating quotes, the silly videos, the news updates. I post pictures of my family and maintain my professional sites. I love looking at photos, peeking into people's lives and seeing what they're up to—or, at least, seeing the version of their lives they want to project to the world.

People, we aren't stupid! We aren't naïve. We hold a collective understanding that social media is a platform on which people can share the very best version of themselves, carefully crafting the image of "living my best life". I'm not judging. I do it too! Not that long ago, I posted a photo of myself sitting all namaste-style in a rainbow field of tulips. It looked gorgeous and serene. My intention was to encourage others to slow down and appreciate the world around us—which is breathtaking and easily taken for granted. Slowing your pace and practicing gratitude is beneficial for your mental health. I still stand by that message although I recognize it's often easier said than done. What the photo *does not* reveal are the hordes of tourists my husband and I had to push through, elbows up, to get the shot. It does not show the tulips that lay limp and damaged, ravaged and trampled on by the thousands of visitors, all trying to achieve the same social media post.

Yes, behind every post is someone's stack of unpaid bills, screaming child, mountain of dirty laundry (literal and figurative), angry spouse or boring job. Everything is staged. And we know it. And we still love it.

Despite this overt trickery, we scroll through our feeds and we can't help that a little jealousy seeps through our pores. *That family looks happy. That vacation looks glamorous. That person is killing it professionally. They all seem happier than I am.*

How can they afford that lifestyle, and I can't? Why does that couple seem so in love and my marriage is struggling? Why are their children doing charity work and mine won't get off their damn cellphones?

This is the voice of fear. It's the voice that whispers hints of failure and doubt. *Am I working hard enough? Am I a good enough spouse? A good mother? Am I living my best life?*

Social media is not the only culprit who induces the voice of fear. Think about people who you admire in your life, either personally or professionally. We love them and look up to them because they inspire us to be better people. However, is there a small piece of you that questions your own validity in comparison?

No? Is it just me?

Alright. I'll go first and give you two examples. Maybe by going first, I will ease your discomfort with the idea that we are often envious of those we love most. (I never said self-reflection would be flattering.)

One of my closest girlfriends is literally the kindest human I know. I would describe her as a bubbling champagne flute of joy. People are drawn to her positive attitude and selfless nature. Her house is always brimming with friends and children, laughing and enjoying life. She is the first person to help you when you are down, to donate to the needy, to babysit your children, to buy you a coffee or to organize a charity event. She is the kind of friend who you could call in the middle of the night with a crisis, big or small, and she would be on your doorstep in five minutes, no questions asked. (Most likely with a bottle of wine in hand.)

Having known her for almost my whole life, I see her flaws. I know she isn't perfect, but she is pretty damn close. Every day, I am grateful she loves me, and our relationship inspires me to be kinder to others. I look up to her enormously. Her marriage is strong. She is the glue that holds her family together. She is thoughtful. No matter what life throws at her, she handles it with grace and wisdom. People adore her, and her social circle is huge.

Beside her, I feel socially awkward and small sometimes. I am not super outgoing by nature. I can also be melodramatic, cynical and selfish. *Is this why I don't have as many friends? Am I not kind enough? Does her light shimmer with more inner beauty than mine? Can someone learn to be more charismatic and at ease? Or am I destined to lack these traits and carry this personality affliction forever?*

It may sound like jealousy, but it's fear. This fear isn't present all of the time—but once in a while, I am awed by her and feel as if I am standing in her shadow. I fear I am a lesser version of her. I fear I am not enough. I fear I am not capable of connecting with others on a meaningful level. I fear I don't laugh enough or smile enough. I fear I will never be loved, as she is.

There is another strong woman on the periphery of my life, someone I admire professionally. While she is not part of my inner circle, she is a fellow educator who I have known for years. In fact, I first met her when I was 11 years old and she was 12. Despite the fact we had a lot in common as kids (and even as adults), we have never been close. In high school, we travelled in different social circles and as adults, we have only had the opportunity to collaborate professionally a handful of times.

We are both teachers, and while at first our careers followed a similar path, hers soon began to eclipse mine. By the time she was 40 years old, she became a principal—one who was greatly admired for being fun, fresh and innovative. Students, teachers, parents and fellow administrators sang her praises.

Now, I had the opportunity to follow this professional path, but chose instead to pursue my passion for writing and public speaking. I consciously decided I did not want to be a principal. It wasn't my calling. However, I'd be lying if I said I wasn't a teensy bit jealous when I heard of her promotion. *A principal at 40? That's very impressive! Had I made the wrong professional choice? Was I missing out on prestige, power and financial security?* FEAR! (And, as a side note, all terrible reasons to become a principal!)

That's not all, my friends.

Not only is this ambitious woman a vivacious and inspiring leader in the field of education, but she is also drop-dead gorgeous! Literally. She's a model in her spare time! She also plays in a band, has a close circle of girlfriends, hosts lavish parties with clever themes, travels the world, and has a long-lasting marriage. Oh, and she's also a mother!

How do I know all of this? Because I stalk her on social media. (The irony is not lost on me ...)

The logical side of my brain knows her life can't possibly be as perfect as it seems. I know principals work long hours, meaning she probably isn't at home as much as she would like. I've heard that, due to demanding schedules of life and work, her band doesn't perform as much as they used to. Everyone makes sacrifices. No one is immune. I know this, yet, the emotional side of my brain measures my success against hers. *How can she accomplish so much? Where does she find the time? The energy? She seems so happy, while I am working my ass off, exhausted and struggling. What am I doing wrong?* Fear.

Ironically, I am aware of how I have been perceived by others. It sounds obnoxious, but my image was intentional. In the past, I have carefully crafted an exterior which appears as if I have it all together. I am a mother, a writer, an educator, a friend, a daughter, a sister, a wife ... I have worked hard to establish a successful career. I spend hours doing yoga or running the streets, sweating like crazy to keep in shape. I rarely leave the house without makeup and a cute outfit. My Game Face says, "I've got this!"

As I get older, I am realizing true power resides in authenticity, and in sharing your messy side as well as your perfection. Meaningful conversations blossom in honest and vulnerable moments. True strength and bravery come from owning your bullshit! This is all easier said than done. Sharing the truest parts of yourself means you need to be comfortable with the good as well as the bad. You need to trust those around you to hold and accept your less-than-beautiful self. Or maybe, you need to learn that all aspects of yourself are, in fact, beautiful and sacred—warts and all.

The Game Face is a mask that hides my fear, my mess, my doubt and my insecurity. It's a defense mechanism I learned early in life—one that served me for a while, but it eventually became a prison I am working to break free from. Having to appear "together" all the time jailed my authenticity and prevented me from bonding my heart with others in the purest forms of connection. I constantly worried what people would think if they knew I wasn't perfect. It was a prideful fear, as my ego liked the image of me being the all-knowing, calm and competent saviour for others. (It sounds obnoxious as I write it, but the truth is, this fear crippled me for a long time.) So, instead of loving all aspects of myself, I branded my imperfections as ugly and weak, put them in a little box and hid them from the world. It was a lonely existence.

Nearing my 40th birthday, I was researching the concept of self-compassion and coming to terms with the fact I did not possess a single shred of it. As I began to show small acts of kindness and acceptance toward myself, I started to wonder what would happen if I opened up to those around me and was brave enough to accept the compassion and love they offered. I decided to break free of the constraints fear placed upon me and I wrote a book about my clumsy journey toward authenticity and self-acceptance. I wanted to strip away The Game Face and expose the truth about my fears. I put it all out there—on a grand scale for the world to read. *Am I enough? Why am I having panic attacks? Who am I without the roles I play?*

My marriage is complex—what does that mean? My brother is an addict—will people judge me for that?

Go big or go home, right?

I wanted to start a conversation about the pressure to appear perfect all the time, the false messages we project, and the implications those choices have on our relationships and mental health. We all have our crosses to bear, our baggage to haul. Chances are, once we're willing to communicate with vulnerability and honesty, we'll discover I am not happier than you and you are not happier than me. We are all simply navigating the complexities of life to the best of our abilities.

Not long after the book was published, a colleague approached, asking for a moment of my time. She is quite a bit younger than me, and isn't someone I had worked closely with before, or socialized with after hours. Our relationship generally consisted of polite smiles, waves and quick greetings in the hallway. Needless to say, I was immediately intrigued by her request.

It turns out, she had recently read my book and was shocked to discover I have a brother who is an addict and has been homeless from time to time. My public admission gave my colleague permission to share her own burden, her own shame. Bravely, she told me of her own brother, who had also been homeless. She whispered she had never been comfortable sharing this struggle before, fearing judgment from others. With honesty, she told me I was the last person she thought she would share this similar history with.

"You always look so happy and well put together, walking down the hall with your friendly smile and your high heels," she told me, "I had no idea you and I have this in common."

I had no idea that's how people saw me—as unapproachable. In my efforts to seem as if I had it all together, the only thing I succeeded in doing was alienating those around me. My desire to appear perfect created a wall which made me untouchable. It was a shocking realization. I had never thought of myself as fake, only private. For most of my life, I hadn't felt comfortable sharing my struggles because I was so concerned about being perceived as a complainer or a downer. What I failed to realize is no one can be bright and shiny all of the time. Admitting to a bad day or a difficult moment is not a party-pooper mentality. It's real life.

As soon as I let go of fear, became open with my struggles, and revealed my authentic self, I shattered the lie that fear told, "You are better than or happier than me."

Rising above my fear and allowing myself to be seen as less than perfect is what gave my colleague the bravery to seek connection. I am so thankful she was courageous enough to climb over my wall of protection and share something so intimate. I'm also grateful I was finally gifted with the wisdom to see myself through her lens. The fact I had admitted publicly to being a hot mess is what made me more accessible. Since that moment, whenever I am invited to speak at an event, write an article, or I see a friend suffering, I make a conscious choice to lead with my imperfections. We are, after all, a shared humanity. We all suffer. We all fail. We all make mistakes. When we rise above the fear of being judged or appearing less than, we create room for meaningful conversation.

Not everyone wants to broadcast their struggles to the world, as I did. (That's slightly insane, I know!) I'm sure you get the message. If you let fear trick you into believing you are less than, you will miss out on the opportunity to connect with others. If you feel like your friends, coworkers, or family members are happier or more successful, chances are they may feel that way about you.

What the Warrior Says:

LESSON 1:
LET GO OF FEAR AND LOOK FOR INSPIRATION.

"Screw comparison! Each one of us is glorious and unique. And, screw my use of the cliche. I say it because it's true. We are all different. We need to own who we are, and celebrate who we are. Differences serve a purpose, for they point out areas in which we may need to grow. You want to be more like her? That's fine. Refine those skills and become a better version of you, but don't you dare negate the woman you already are."

My girlfriend, the one I told you about earlier, is as glorious and warm as the sunshine on a July afternoon. Yes, she is friendlier than I am, more outgoing and probably kinder too. I admire her for that. However, there are things she admires about me as well. I am incredibly hardworking and ambitious. I am calm, loyal and supportive. I am willing to take risks to follow my dreams. We both stand proudly and compensate for each other.

She reminds me to laugh and have fun. I calm her worries about parenting and all of life's uncertainties. We need each other, and our differences push the other to become better, stronger.

While I greatly admire my colleague for her professional and personal dedications, I realize I do not wish to emulate her career. I appreciate her leadership, but I choose to inspire others in a different way. One way is not better than the other. We all have dreams and follow them to the best of our ability.

Fear made me jealous of other women and left me feeling less than. Yet, when I chose to let go of fear and rise above my insecurity, I became inspired by them—to be kind, to be innovative, and to live a life of passion and adventure.

Surround yourself with great people whose strengths you can learn from and who can encourage you to grow. It may seem scary to spend time with people who intimidate you or who trigger insecurities, but if you are constantly the best person in the room, who is pushing you to become better? And while a certain level of discomfort is normal—good even—never forget you are amazing too. In your own way, you add color to the lives of others, just as they do to yours.

LESSON 2:
IF YOU MEASURE YOURSELF AGAINST OTHERS, YOU WILL USUALLY FALL SHORT.

"We all look bright and shiny from the outside, but underneath that superficial sheen, most of us are a hot mess. Very few of us are willing to show our dark or messy sides, so don't buy into someone's

public persona. Get up close and personal, where you can see the dirt beneath the polish. That's where humanity is."

In his book, "The 7 Laws of Spiritual Success", Deepak Chopra writes about the dangers of referencing others rather than referencing ourselves. While we can certainly look to others for guidance, support, encouragement or inspiration, we should be wary of measuring our own success on someone else's terms.

Social media makes it incredibly easy to fall into this trap. *He has a nicer car than me. They go on more vacations than I do. She takes her kids on so many adventures and is clearly a better mother than I am.* Social comparison is a breeding ground for fear. Fear that we are not enough. That we are missing out. That others are happier than we are.

This feels like an opportune moment to remind you we are rarely privy to what happens behind closed doors. Perhaps that new car was bought on credit and he is one late payment away from financial catastrophe. Maybe that family vacations a lot because their daily schedule is insane. They are overworked, overstressed and don't spend much time together at home. Those beautiful children, adventuring with their mother could have erupted into a full-scale meltdown after the photo was snapped.

Instead of looking to others to judge the quality of your life, could it be possible to measure your own success and happiness by looking within?

Read that sentence again. It's a game changer.

After all, not everyone shares the same definition of success. Some people value love and friendship. Others long for professional accolades and financial security. Ask yourself, do I *need* a nice car to feel successful? Do I *need* a large circle of friends to feel loved? How important is my career? Does my life have balance? Am I doing my very best as a spouse? Parent? Friend? What makes one person feel fulfilled may be different than the next. Not only is that okay, it's freaking awesome! It's how we learn from one another and become exposed to varying perspectives and life experiences. If you are only looking at the achievements of others, how will you know what truly fulfills you?

And so, my friends, when fear (disguised as jealousy) rears its ugly head, and tells you others are happier and more successful, take a moment to take stock of your own life. Look within and evaluate the areas of your life that bring you joy and acknowledge the ones that require your focus. Without a doubt, you will find things that need improvement, things that need attention and things that need to change. This does not mean you are less than anyone around you. Every single human on this planet has aspects of their lives that call for growth. Be proud you are self-aware enough to see the need for change. Then, go for it!

THEIR LIVES ARE BETTER THAN MINE

"Refine those skills and become a better version of you, but don't you dare negate the woman you already are."

1. Who do you admire?

2. How do they inspire you to be a better version of yourself?

3. What stories are you telling yourself that make your life seem *less than*?

4. If your life remained exactly as-is, could you make peace with it? If not, what needs to change?

Chapter 2

FEAR SAYS:
"THE BRIGHT SIDE
IS THE ONLY SIDE"

My grandmother is dying. She hasn't lived an easy life, but it's had some wonderful moments. She escaped her abusive childhood by getting married the day after her 18th birthday. She had a child a year later and spent the next 60 years of marriage caring for her husband and three children. When I was young, we used to vacation at her house for one week every summer. My mother, siblings and I would fly from small-town Alberta and enjoy an adventure in the big, gorgeous city of Vancouver. My grandma was fun. She would take us to the beach, where we could build sandcastles and watch the waves crash upon the shore. We would collect seashells and count the ocean liners on the horizon. We would go to the annual fair and stay up late, listening to live music, our fingers sticky with popcorn butter and cotton candy. Even her small, cozy house felt like a wonderland. She had bunk beds to climb on, a hammock in the yard and a pool table in the basement. There were snacks my mother would never give us at home, food which I will eternally associate with my grandma—prunes, chocolate chip cookies and Cheez Whiz on white bread. It was my favourite week of the summer.

Eventually, my family moved to Vancouver and we got to see my grandmother more often. She became a staple in our lives. When my siblings and I were teenagers—moody and irritable—other family members pulled away, not knowing how to deal with our sullen faces and disconnected demeanor. My grandmother, though, always found a way to connect. She continued to show up at our sporting events, with a bag of freshly baked cookies in hand. She would watch every play, every recital, every speech. Even now, she reads every article and book I write. She looks at pictures of my children and loves to hear silly stories about them. She is and always has been genuinely interested in our lives. She is a sweet, positive and gentle person to be around.

She is also the first person to admit that getting old sucks. While her mind has been sharp, her body has been failing her for years. Lupus has ravaged her immune system and arthritis has crippled her hands, turning them into gnarled, painful appendages. Her skin bruises and bleeds at the slightest touch. Unsteady on her feet, she shuffles along, often catching her slippers on the carpet, tumbling every now and then. Sidewalk curbs and stairs present a challenge. Automatic doors and crosswalk countdowns seem too quick for her slow-moving body. She fought using a walker for the longest time as she didn't want to appear old. She wasn't ready to be elderly. But age catches up with us all, despite our best efforts to hide from it.

My grandmother has been waging war against her failing body for some time, and now, she is tired. Her heart is weakening and every moment, every breath, is a struggle. I went to visit her this morning, in the hospital facility where she is waiting to die. I have visited her many times in the various facilities she has lived in over the last few years. No matter how terrible she felt that day, she always managed to straighten her back, put on a smile and express gratitude for the effort I made to see her. Not today, though. Today, I saw her suffering. Papery skin covered her skeletal body, which was swollen in strange places—fluid gathering is a sign of failing circulation and congestive heart failure. Her breath was raspy, laborious. Her eyes closed, fighting off pain and focusing on taking each breath, in and out. She couldn't listen to the stories I told her, and didn't enjoy the photos I showed her. She was present in body, but not in mind or spirit. I stayed a short while only, worried the effort of my visit would exhaust her.

I left the hospital and sat in the car in silence, processing what I had seen. My brain and my body were paralyzed by a fact I didn't want to know. There was no denying, she would die soon.

As I get older, I recognize more and more often that difficult emotional moments—such as this one—come with a choice. How will I react? I can choose to focus on the lesson, the silver lining, the bright side. Or I can choose pain and suffering.

Seeing my grandmother in discomfort, knowing it may be our last visit, was shocking and deeply sad. I knew she was ready to go. Her body and spirit were tired of fighting. Death would release her from pain, from a life which no longer brought her joy. At that moment, I decided to accept my grandmother's impending death and be grateful her struggle would soon end.

When I arrived home that afternoon, my husband, Miguel—sensing an emotional struggle within me and knowing my morning had been a difficult one—reached out with love and empathy.

"How are you doing, mi amor? How do you feel?" he asked.

"I don't want to talk about it."

Talking about it would only serve to stir up the sorrow brewing inside me. I didn't want to feel pain. I had decided to focus on the bright side instead of wallowing in the sadness. I am strong and I understand the natural progression of life. Death is inevitable and I needed to be okay with this impending loss.

Respecting my choice to process this alone, my lovely husband sat with me, holding my hand. After some time, he tentatively broke the silence.

"I know this hasn't been an easy day for you. Let me take you out for lunch. I'll buy you a burger," he offered, knowing it is my favorite food and will very possibly be the meal I will request on my own deathbed.

My response to his kind and caring offer? I broke. All strength, and the resolve to be positive left my body and I sobbed hysterically! "That … is … so … nice of you!" I blubbered, mascara painting black tears down my face.

He held me and patiently let me cry, then made a cautious, yet astute observation, "I'm guessing this reaction is not about the hamburger?"

Here's the thing, folks. I have always prided myself on being "strong enough" to find the positive in any difficult situation. I am a glass-half-full kind of girl. Yet, sometimes—actually many times—this pressure to be hopeful and to trust The Universe's plan causes me to disregard any negative or uncomfortable feelings. Had I just taken a hot minute to admit I was sad, the whole "Hamburger Debacle" could have been avoided. My grandmother was dying, for cripes' sake! Why couldn't I allow myself a moment of sorrow?

From this story, you would never know I've been in therapy to deal with my discomfort of emotions which I deem to be "negative". (Not to discount the amazing work of my incredible counselor. I would be lost without him. Old habits die hard, I suppose, and mine seem especially difficult to break.) You would also never know, in my professional life, I am passionate about supporting and developing emotional intelligence. (Do as I say and not as I do, right?) Actually, I believe my own struggles make me better at my job. I can speak about emotional discomfort, anxiety and depression because I live it. I fight it. And, some days, I rise above it.

I am in therapy because my attempts to manipulate life and control The Universe are the source of my depression. My need to feel positive, hopeful and happy are obsessive and cause me to disregard and ignore any emotion that threatens the image of the strong, grateful woman I want to project. It's not as simple as sweeping emotions under the rug. I fear them. I fear sadness, regret, anger, jealousy, and helplessness. I flat out refuse to acknowledge their existence in my emotional repertoire. I've become pretty good at evading them, dodging uncomfortable emotions like Keanu Reeves dodging bullets in the movie, "The Matrix". Yet, they always seem to catch up with me.

While my brain refuses to acknowledge stress, my body soaks it up like a sponge. For me, ignoring my true feelings has resulted in stomach aches, lethargy, and mind- numbing insomnia. For you, stress may appear as migraine headaches, a lack of motivation, or a short temper. Just because you choose to ignore something does not mean it goes away. (Although I have wished upon many a star it would.) Along with physical symptoms, my efforts to put a lid on negativity has caused the occasional emotional eruption. In the past, despite my best efforts to control my feelings, anger would seep out—like a leak in a dam—usually directed, irrationally, at something totally unrelated to what I was actually upset about. Does that ever happen to you? No? Just me? Let's unpack this a little further.

Among the lengthy list of emotions I like to ignore, stress is at the top. I pride myself on being the girl who can do it all. My work keeps me incredibly busy, yet I am the first one to pick up another project. I show up at every single soccer game to watch my kids. I help them study for their exams at school. I make healthy lunches and dinners for the family. I am there when my girlfriends have a moment of crisis. I plan the next social gathering. I make sure I have time to work out so I feel physically fit and strong. I leave love notes for my husband so he feels appreciated. Do I need help? No! I am so bloody organized! I've got this. Except now, every minute of every day is scheduled.

I once explained my rigorous self-care routine to my therapist. Every day, I wake up at 5am to meditate. I write in my gratitude journal and do yoga. After work, I make sure I have at least 30 minutes to run before returning to the chaos of my family. On a regular basis, I listen to podcasts and read books about personal growth. I said all of this with pride, waiting for my therapist to praise my efforts. Gold star for me! His response? "Kelly, that sounds exhausting."

The negative consequences of my "I've got this" attitude is evident when my husband gently suggests my children forgot to do their chores. Instead of agreeing with him (because they did forget!) and reminding my kids to honor their responsibilities, I lose my fucking mind! How dare he question my parenting?! It is my choice as to how I enforce discipline and assign chores! I didn't ask for his opinion, thank you very much! His request for the children to pick up their dirty socks is not unreasonable, yet the dam of repressed stress and frustration bursts and the ensuing flood is now dangerously out of control.

I know it's not about the dirty socks. He knows it's not about the dirty socks. My pent-up emotions simply need an outlet, and he is the unlucky victim. At this moment, when I am yelling, accusing and crying, I know it's an unfair reaction. Ironically, this reaction reinforces my misconception about negative emotions. See? I told you I am not good at expressing anger! I need to work harder to ensure I never feel anger again. (That's messed up, right?) If I had learned to believe that stress is okay, that anger and sorrow are normal, I would have also learned to express them in an appropriate and controlled manner. Instead, I put them in a little box, place them on a shelf and never look in that direction again. As charming as this personality trait may seem, this irrational behavior began to take its toll on my marriage. Miguel's patience with my lack of emotional intelligence began to fade—and rightfully so. One can only stand calmly in the storm for so long before retreating. I needed to face my fear of uncomfortable feelings. Hence, therapy.

I hate it when therapists want to delve into your childhood. I am a grown-ass woman. Despite our childhoods, I believe everyone needs to take ownership of who they are today. I can sympathize with those of you who survived a traumatic upbringing. I won't ever judge the impact that had on you. However, I might gently suggest there comes a time when we need to stop blaming our shortcomings on our parents. In order to heal, we need to own our flaws and realize we are in full control of who we choose to be in this world as an adult. The thought is empowering, really.

I recognize all parents inflict some damage on their children, no matter how well intentioned they may be. It's a natural part of life. Parents are flawed people (just like the rest of us) who are slogging through their emotional issues while attempting to perform the hardest task known to man—raise tiny humans. Knowing how flawed and imperfect I am, my attitude toward therapy and childhood explorations is perhaps a defense mechanism. Accepting the idea that my childhood holds hints to the root cause of my anxiety inevitably implies I am currently in the process of scarring my own children and will be the cause of their future therapy sessions.

I had an amazing childhood and am the first to tell my therapist he is wading into waters which hold no deep, dark secrets. My parents coached my baseball team, watched my theater performances and raised me to chase my dreams. We had family dinner every Sunday. We went camping, vacationed in Hawaii and, most importantly, I felt loved. My childhood was safe and comfortable. I have always felt very lucky and am quick to defend my parents. They did a bang-up job! I am a successful, thriving adult as a result of their hard work and care. Ignoring my objections, my therapist wanted to start at the beginning.

"Tell me about the quality of conversation in your household. Was it meaningful? Did you feel safe to openly express and discuss your feelings?" he inquired in one of our early sessions.

Huh. Um ... (Can you hear the crickets chirping?)

Let me preface my answer by saying my parents did the very best job they could. They too, are products of how they were raised. My mom and dad were both raised in a generation where children were to be seen and not heard. And feelings? Well, you didn't talk about that stuff. Feelings were private, not to be shared or pondered and most of all, not to be discussed. I feel the conflicting needs to be honest with you about my childhood experiences, but also wish to convey my past with the utmost respect for the lovely humans who raised me. I lay no blame, for I take ownership of my struggles. My adversity is both experienced by, and created by, me alone. It's true, some challenges are a result of the way I perceived emotional moments in my childhood. That, I can't deny. However, perception seems to be the key word here. Every story I share is neither the truth nor the untruth. It is simply my past, as I remember it. However accurate—or inaccurate—my recollections may be, is irrelevant, because the emotional imprinting that resulted has shaped me to be who I am today. For better or for worse.

Asking me to sum up my early, developmental relationship with emotions may seem to be an immense, complex task. Impossible to do, you might think, yet, I can do it in two words: Game Face. I don't know where that term came from, whether I adopted it all on my own, or subconsciously picked it up along the way.

I come from a family of athletes who pride themselves on being tough—physically and mentally resilient. My dad was an all-around athlete, excelling in every sport he attempted: track and field, soccer, downhill skiing, hockey. My mom is an excellent track athlete herself and also a volleyball player. Sports played an enormous role in our family culture, my siblings and I all reaching highly-competitive levels in our chosen activities.

My parents watched every game and coached us for many years. It makes sense that "Game Face" is a term used to describe an athlete's focus, dedication and determination. The best athletes push through pain and adversity, keeping their eyes on the prize. For me, however, the term took on a life of its own and morphed into an enigma which skewed my view of people in my family, difficult conversations, and how emotions were valued or accepted in my family.

The truth is, I don't recall having meaningful conversation as a child. Don't get me wrong, my family spoke every day and (for the most part) we enjoyed each other's company. We talked about our daily activities, friends, school and sports, amongst other things. We laughed and we fought, like other families. In fact, we fought a lot. My sister and I were often like oil and water, a raging, hysterical ball of hormones. From a young age, and continuing into our adolescent years, we just didn't connect and did very little to try and understand each other. This lack of understanding easily crossed over into resentment and we would scream, cry and even become violent with one another over the smallest perceived slight. My mother, struggling to remain calm in the midst of it all, was often sucked into the vortex of dysregulation, succumbing to her own stress and anxiety. In these estrogen-induced battles, one message came ringing through loud and clear—this is not normal. Do not let anyone know we behave like this. Our household adopted the same slogan as Vegas. And, appropriately, Fight Club. You all know it. *What happens in our house, stays in our house.*

When we left the house, we did so as a calm and caring family unit. Put all of your bullshit in a box so no one sees it and pretend—at least for two hours—that you get along. Game Face.

You see, anger, sorrow, and frustration are acceptable emotions as long as they do not become an inconvenience or make others uncomfortable. No one wants to be around someone who is a downer. No one really wants to hear about your struggles. As a result, when someone asks how you are, the answer is *always* a positive one, even if it is not true. After all, there must be *something* happy or exciting you can share about your life. My translation? These negative emotions are not only unwanted and unwelcome, they make you unlovable and weak.

Let me reiterate. This message was never explicitly said to me by anyone. It was the underlying message I perceived from the adults around me.

In my childhood home, there was never an open display of uncomfortable emotions. For instance, I never saw my parents argue but I could feel their stress—even as a small child. When we were young, my dad lost his job and, subsequently, my parents lost their house. Yet, I don't ever recall a tense conversation, much less an open argument. That was all behind closed doors. But I knew times were tough because I can remember my mother going grocery shopping with a calculator because she only had the money in her hand to spend. The first time I saw my dad cry was when I was 14 years old and his father died. Before that, tears from any man in my life were unseen and unheard of. This show of emotion was shocking and I had no idea how to comfort him. My idol growing up was my dad's mother, who was a stoic pillar of strength. She was regal, opinionated, and well-respected by all members of our family. She, like the rest of us, maintained a stiff upper lip upon the passing of her husband, which served to reinforce the message that grief is private. You may weep in the privacy of your home, but when with others, strength and leadership is what is needed, what is respected.

All of the adults around—with the exception of my mother who had the occasional (and understandable!) emotional release—were calm and "in control" of their feelings, very rarely expressing sadness or temper. I say "in control" for I am certain it is code for "repression". I was too young and naïve to understand the concept of repression. I took things at face value and decided being "in control" of your emotions is what made you strong. So, I became a young woman who was ambitious, charming, sociable, and "happy". To admit I was tired, overwhelmed, lonely and uncertain would be to expose my weaknesses. This was not an option, and I began to fear any emotion that could make me a less-likeable person.

What I didn't learn until much, much later in life is that emotional repression is dangerous and isolating.

When we open our hearts and minds to look for messages from The Universe, cosmic signs inevitably appear. In my case, I received two strong suggestions that it was time to get over my fear of negative emotions and bury The Game Face forever. (In truth, there were probably more messages than just two, but these are the ones I picked up on. I giggle now, thinking about The Universe, persistent but losing patience with me. "I need to send *another one*? Come on, girl! When are you going to get this?!")

A few years ago, I was suffering from debilitating stomach pain. Some days, it was a dull ache that would last for 8 to 12 hours. Other times, it felt like a sharp stabbing in the gut—fetal-position stuff. I tried acupuncture, diet changes, holistic medication and any other solution I could think of to feel better, but to no avail. Miguel had been nagging me for months to seek proper medical advice, but I am always hesitant to visit busy clinic doctors who listen to you for 30 seconds and write a prescription. This exact scenario had occurred the summer before when I took ulcer medication every day for three months before discovering I did not have an ulcer. To add salt to the wound, the doctor stated firmly I was not to drink a drop of alcohol while on this medication. I wasted a whole summer, swallowing three horse-sized pills a day, without so much as a margarita. I didn't even lick one salted rim. A whole summer with no booze people! And to find out it was all a misdiagnosis?! You can imagine my disdain. Nope, no clinic doctors for me. Instead, like every self-diagnosing idiot on the planet, I Googled my symptoms. The most likely cause of my pain: cancer.

Sorry, what now?! Off to the doctor I went, bracing myself for serious news. How would I break it to my children? My parents would be devastated. As I mentally practiced the inevitable (and heartbreaking) conversations that would follow this appointment, the doctor came into the office—her body language relatively relaxed and casual for this impending doom.

"How's your stress level?" she asked. "Are you sleeping at night?"

"My stress level is fine," I replied, "and I never sleep well. It's been that way for years."

"What's going on in your life, lately?"

"Well, I have cancer." (That's what I wanted to say, but recognized it should be her delivery, not mine.) "Um, I went back to university recently. My husband also lost his job a few months ago. We're struggling a little bit with our youngest child. And I don't think I like my day job anymore."

At that point, my doctor literally laughed out loud and quickly smothered her giggle. Nice recovery. "And, you think your stress level is fine? Honey, you don't need me, you need to see a therapist." (This was in pre-therapy days, obviously.)

The thing is, I honestly thought I was handling everything fine. Really! I had acknowledged my family's adversities, but felt a strong conviction to focus on the things we *did* have going for us—our kids were healthy, we had a nice home and we loved each other.

My doctor explained further, "If your mind refuses to accept and deal with stress, your body hangs on to it. Stress won't magically disappear. You need to do the work necessary to deal with it in a healthy way. Ignoring it only brings suffering."

I slunk away, tail between my legs, feeling simultaneously relieved and embarrassed. I knew something had to change. It seemed I needed to put my big-girl panties on and face my fear about uncomfortable emotions. The second sign came a few weeks later.

The messengers who opened my eyes once and for all, were my sweet, sweet children. There was a time when I had two biological children, one stepson, and one enormous fur-baby—a 130lb Bernese Mountain Dog named Don Julio. (Yes, we named him after a bottle of tequila.) Don Julio brought an incredible amount of joy to our family. He was all beauty and no brains but he had the loveliest disposition of any dog I have ever come across. He would wrestle with the boys, but always let them win, never letting on that he could pin them with one gigantic paw. Knowing and obeying the rule that he was not allowed on the furniture—but wanting desperately to cuddle with the family—he would rest his monstrous head on my lap and gaze up at us with his golden puppy eyes, wide, round, and heart-melting. One paw would inch its way onto my lap, then another, until half his body sprawled across mine. He would always keep at least one foot on the floor, to "technically" follow the rules. "I'm not resting on the couch. See?"

At the time, I was teaching at an inner-city school and had the privilege of spending my days educating and caring for children from impoverished, difficult (and sometimes devastating) backgrounds. Their emotional needs often exceeded their ability to learn and I found myself acting as their counselor, their caretaker, and their protector—as well as their teacher. Due to the extraordinary needs of our school community, we attracted an incredible staff of innovative educators, all willing to think outside the box and go the extra mile to serve our students. Don Julio often came to school with me. His gentle and calm nature had a ripple effect in my classroom. He would lounge beside my desk as children (who would normally refuse to read) shared book after book with him. My students would bury their faces in his soft fur and tell him their deepest worries, knowing he would keep their secrets and hold their big emotions with acceptance and grace. He taught these children how to care for another living thing and demonstrated what unconditional love looks like. Don Julio quickly became the most popular staff member at our school.

However, even when things are close to perfect, they rarely stay the same. Life calls for change and I was posted to work at a new school. This school was in a more affluent neighborhood and closer to my home, and would reduce both my commute and my stress level. Working at an inner-city school was one of the great gifts of my life but also made my heart bleed. After years of service, I felt emotionally depleted and needed a change. My new school presented a more traditional environment and was not as progressive as my previous place of employment. Don Julio was forced into retirement, as he was not welcome to spend his time lounging in my new classroom. My sweet fur-baby, who was used to being around children 24 hours a day, was now relegated to spend his days alone, in our home, while his family went to work and to school. Very quickly, his demeanor changed. He became anxious, misbehaving often. My heart broke for him. He wasn't naughty. He was lonely.

Around this time, one of Miguel's colleagues experienced the devastating loss of her dog, who passed due to a seizure. Knowing we were animal lovers, she shared her grief with him and asked if he knew where she could find another dog. This woman worked from home and lived on a sprawling 5 acre piece of property. She trained her dogs as expert trackers and took them hiking in the woods every day. When Miguel returned home that evening, he tentatively broached the idea of sending Don Julio to live with her. My initial reaction wasn't pretty. It was emotional and selfish.

"How dare you suggest we give him away! He is a member of our family, often my *favorite* member of the family! I cannot believe you would be so coldhearted! Would you give away one of our children?"

Miguel continued, reminding me to consider Don Julio's current quality of life. What do we want *for him*? At our home, he was alone for 8 to 10 hours a day, moping around, waiting for his family to return. When we came home, he jumped in the back of our vehicle and was shuttled around to soccer practice, track and field events, and music lessons. Alternatively, this woman could offer Don Julio an enormous yard to explore. There, he would be able to run wild and free. She had another dog, Lennon, who would be Don Julio's companion and playmate.

She had no children of her own and no spouse. Her dogs were her life and had her whole heart.

Dammit. There was no doubt. This was the right choice—as much as I didn't want it to be. However, Miguel and I agreed the final decision needed to come from my kids. He was, after all, their best friend too.

We sat down with the boys the next evening and told them our concerns.

"Don Julio isn't happy here. We all love him so much, but we can't provide him with the life he deserves."

We told them about Miguel's friend, her dogs and her farm, then asked them to share their thoughts on the situation. There are moments, as a parent, when you get to see the fruits of your labor, when your children display such selflessness and courage that you know, beyond a shadow of a doubt, you are raising them well. This was such a moment.

After sitting in silence for a minute or two, my youngest, who is the most passionate animal lover of all of us, spoke, "Don Julio would be happier there than he is with us."

So, we agreed. The hard choice was the right choice. It would break our hearts, but it was a decision based in love.

I looked into the faces of my children and saw the pain in their eyes. Yet, they remained stoic, staring straight back at me. I knew the look on their faces. I invented that look. My boys, hearts shattered on the inside, knowing they had to say goodbye to something they loved, were pushing their feelings down and trying to remain strong. They wore The Game Face.

Oh my God, I've done it to them! I have modeled for them, exactly what was shown to me as a child. Sadness, anger, and fear are signs of weakness and are never to be shared with others. I couldn't believe I had raised my boys to hold those same emotional understandings. In an instant, my mind flashed back to all of the times I allowed this belief to be cultivated in my own home. I remembered sending my toddlers to their rooms for a timeout, telling them they were welcome to come out only when they were capable of being happy and kind. I recalled scraped knees and a mother telling her sons, "It's not so bad. You're fine." I saw all the times when I cried in my shower, so I didn't expose my children to sadness. I should have cried in front of them, showing them that tears are normal and acceptable. I should have modeled the strategies I use to calm myself in moments of anger or sorrow. I should have shown them how to comfort someone who is sad or frustrated, instead of sheltering them from pain and big feelings. Nope, I didn't do any of those things. Instead, I showed them how to wear The Game Face.

Right there, in the midst of this family meeting, I knew, unequivocally, it was time to change—not only for my own sake, but also for my children.

"You know, when I first thought about giving Don Julio away, I cried about it. I cried a lot. Do you feel like you need to cry?"

Little chins quivered, pouty lips trembled, and their eyes filled with tears. Together, for the first time, Miguel and I cried with my children. In fact, we sobbed. It was magical.

What the Warrior Says:

LESSON 1:
THERE ARE NO SUCH THINGS AS "NEGATIVE" EMOTIONS.

"Having feelings makes you a well-rounded human. No one is happy 100% of the time. If you are, it's bullshit. Constant glitter and rainbows are fake. Fake is a form of cowardice because you are not being brave enough to own who you are."

"You thought the word 'aggressive' was negative. It can be. It can also be fierce, in a 'hell-yeah' kind of way. Pain can be negative if you let it limit your possibilities. Or pain can become your fuel. Anger can paralyze you. Or it can drive you. Emotions aren't negative. They're necessary."

The word "negative" in and of itself carries heavy implications, doesn't it? Negative. Terrible. Bad. Are any of our feelings bad? Does having negative emotions make you a bad person? Okay, admittedly, I may not be the best person to ask. I clearly have a messed up relationship with my feelings and was raised with the clichéd British "stiff upper lip". But cut me some slack! I am working my ass off to redefine my core beliefs and it's not easy.

I have thrown the word "negative" out with the trash and have chosen, instead, to adopt the word "uncomfortable". While I fear negativity, I don't fear discomfort. Discomfort is the breeding ground for growth. Discomfort is the first step toward evolution and change. I lean into discomfort, for I know that pushing through it will make me a better person. I never want to be associated with the word, "negative" but I can make peace with "uncomfortable".

I have learned all emotions are valid and deserve some attention. There is nothing wrong with being angry, frustrated or sad, as long as we express those feelings with a little bit of grace and dignity. Simply acknowledging those feelings and observing them immediately strips their power. (Quick flashback to the Great Hamburger Debacle.) If I had simply noticed my sadness and been okay with not being okay, the festering build-up would have been exponentially less dramatic. Now, when experiencing an uncomfortable emotion, I fight hard against this habit. Instead of quickly pushing that emotion aside, I have learned to sit with it, to let it have a presence. I ride the wave, knowing the waters will calm once again.

For years, I brushed "negative" feelings under the rug and chose to ignore them. It was easier, less scary. If I ignored those pesky feelings, they couldn't threaten my sense of self or my need to be bright and shiny. The problem is those feelings never go away, even when left unattended. Especially when left unattended. When you hide too many issues under the rug, you will inevitably trip on them when you least expect it. I pushed down so many uncomfortable emotions that eventually the well would overflow. Perhaps you might see yourself in the following scenario. Take solace in the fact you are not alone. Loss of control happens to the best of us.

My life often leaves me overwhelmed, overscheduled, and sleep-deprived. My children, like most, are busy. They can be demanding of my attention, excited to share the triumphs and struggles of their day or to show me something cool on their video games. Their noise level is loud and excitable. I bite my lip, resisting all instinct to unleash the stress of my work day upon them. My smile is plastered, my voice artificially light and carefree. Exhausted, I expertly multitask as I make dinner, listen to my children tell the stories of their day, and help them with their homework. I answer texts and emails—all the while remembering to keep an eye on the chili simmering on the stove. My husband comes home from work and I greet him at the door with a smile and a kiss. He asks how my day was, and I, reluctant to greet him as a run-down and tired wife, reply that it was "productive". We sit down to enjoy supper together and he casually remarks it tastes salty. After dinner he washes the dishes but forgets to put away the condiments, which are forever destined to sit on the kitchen table, unless I, mother and martyr, put them away and I *lose my shit! Must I do everything?!*

If I had only taken a moment to admit I was feeling overwhelmed and asked for help cooking supper, or had taken a quiet moment to regain my balance, this crisis could have been averted.

Feeling overwhelmed is not a sign of weakness. It is a natural state of existence for most working parents. I am learning that admitting how I truly feel is different than complaining. It is authentic and normal. We can learn to observe our feelings without judgment. I can express exhaustion without thinking it makes me a terrible wife or parent. I can forgive myself for being tired and use self-compassion to engage in a self-care practice, enabling me to carry on in brighter spirits.

Imagine a friend of yours calls you expressing she's had a terrible day. Her boss berated her, her children were misbehaving, she burnt dinner, and was late getting her children to music lessons. It was an all-around crappy day and she was left feeling emotionally depleted. Would you tell her she was a failure? Would you shame her for being disorganized and weak? Of course not! You would remind her she is an outstanding human being, who is simply having an off-day, and you would advise her to pour a gigantic glass of wine and have a bubble bath before bed. We so easily express compassion toward others. Why is it so difficult to extend that same kindness to ourselves?

I have also learned that when we refuse to acknowledge "negative" emotions, our positive emotions fade too. Unfortunately, we cannot pick and choose our feelings. (Although, if feelings were a buffet, life would certainly be simpler.) Repression does not discriminate. When we push our feelings down, we are often left with numbness. Devoid of joy as well as sorrow. Learning to sit with uncomfortable feelings instead of pushing them away allows room for positivity as well.

For me, a healthier relationship with my emotions began by simply noticing how I was feeling, both physically and emotionally, and exploring those emotions without judgment. Because I was not adept at detecting stress or anxiety, I would often feel it as a tightness in my chest or a discomfort in my stomach. I would wonder what this was about? What is happening in my life, at this moment, that may be causing me stress? I would mentally scroll through my week, thinking about events that may have been upsetting but didn't register with me emotionally at the time. Then, I would simply take a moment to acknowledge how I was feeling. *"I think I may be carrying some stress because of..."*

In times when emotions were strong and undeniable, I would resist my tendency to push them away and began to give myself time to just let them be. It sounds cheesy, but I would even say it aloud, to myself. *I am feeling frustrated and that's okay. I am going to give myself 10 minutes to feel this before I try to move past it and find the silver lining.* Giving myself permission to be less than okay was powerful. Doing so removed self-judgment and normalized my reactions. Providing a time limit for myself is my own quirky way of combating my fear of marinating in negativity. This tactic fights against my life-long habit of immediately needing to find the positive.

My strategy sounds simplistic, I know. But for an emotionally-stunted human like me, we need to start with the basics. There is power in recognizing and acknowledging pain. It's the first step toward healing and living a healthy emotional life. When I learned to develop emotional self-awareness, the fear I had of uncomfortable feelings began to disappear. It takes practice to find grace in being uncomfortable. The more I practiced, the more confident I became in handling my emotions. My mind and body started to relax, and joy began to show up in small, but unmistakable ways. My brain, which was previously working overtime to hide and disregard my emotions, suddenly became available to notice beauty and wonderment around me. The more I noticed the awesomeness of everyday life, the more gratitude I expressed, and the more positive I became.

Don't believe it can be that easy? Try it for two weeks. Stop pushing away your feelings and simply sit with them for a moment. Talk to yourself as if you would talk to a cherished friend. I swear, this little shift in mentality may just be a game changer.

LESSON 2:
MEANINGFUL RELATIONSHIPS ARE BUILT ON VULNERABILITY.

"Hear me when I say, weakness is not a synonym for vulnerability. Wisdom, strength, bravery. Those are synonyms for vulnerability. Even a warrior takes off her armor at the end of the day."

I am a fairly social person by nature. I have a small, but close, circle of girlfriends, most of whom I have known for years. I am the person who organizes coffee dates, dinner parties and girls' nights out. I am also the person who will listen to your drama, wipe your tears and help you solve the problem. I am not, however, the person who will share my struggles with others. My core belief about the importance of positivity and not wanting to be a downer is a hard one to shake. Here's the irony. I never once thought of my girlfriends as downers when they wanted to talk about their struggles. I was happy to help them and felt privileged they shared with me. I suppose I admired their vulnerability. It was okay for them. Not for me.

About a year ago, when emotional repression was getting the best of me, the people around me began to notice cracks in my shiny surface. Miguel commented he didn't trust my smile because he knew it was a bullshitter's grin, covering up my stress. I had the same conversation with more than one girlfriend. It went somewhat like this:

"Are you okay, Kel? You seem a little stressed."

"I'm fine. Things are just busy and I'm more tired than normal. It's okay. I can handle it."

"You know, it would be okay if you *couldn't* handle it. If you need to vent or cry, it's alright. Actually, it will bring us closer together. I've cried in front of you before, but you have never cried in front of me. When you need to sob, I will be here."

I am a firm believer if The Universe presents you with the same situation multiple times, you need to pull your head out of the sand and listen. After some self-reflection, I realized they were all right. My relationships were fairly one-sided. I always acted as the caretaker, but I never let anyone take care of me. And they wanted to! Allowing people to see me with some authenticity was scary as hell. It made me feel naked and exposed. But by not revealing my authenticity, I made those closest to me feel excluded from my life. Though I didn't mean to, my actions showed that I didn't trust them. I needed to remove the fear that if I let people know how I was truly feeling, they wouldn't like me or want to spend time with me. What I've come to realize, though, is in being vulnerable, people will actually like me more. They no longer need to guess how I am feeling or feel isolated by my false smile, when they know something deeper is going on. One of my girlfriends often says, "I'm not telling you about me, until you talk about yourself first."

Though it's still a challenge for me, I am trying to be authentic in my responses when people ask how I am doing. I am reframing my thinking by distinguishing a difference between complaining and being honest. I am reminding myself that by reaching out to those around me, I create emotional space for connection. And on the days when I say I am feeling amazing, I want people to trust that's how I truly feel and enjoy the moment with me, rather than question it.

So, while I still try to look on the bright side of any given situation, I now understand that before I can find a lesson or engage in self-reflection, I must first go through the following list:

1. Allow myself space to feel any and all emotions, even uncomfortable ones.

2. Remind myself that experiencing uncomfortable emotions does not make me weak.

3. Engage in a self-care practice.

4. Be honest with others and reach out for support.

5. Then, and only then, may I try to move past a challenging moment. I need to wait until the smile is real before I dress everything with a silver lining.

THE BRIGHT SIDE IS THE ONLY SIDE

*"Even a warrior takes off her armor
at the end of the day."*

Make a list of comfortable and uncomfortable emotions.

1. When you experience an uncomfortable emotion, how do you typically react?

2. Can you come up with a new plan of action? How would your Best Self experience and express uncomfortable emotions?

Chapter 3

FEAR SAYS:
"LOVE SHOULD BE EASY"

What do you think happened to Cinderella after the glass slipper slid onto her foot and the prince promptly rescued her from the grips of her evil stepmother? Surely, they had a lavish wedding, with the best gourmet catering and a signature cocktail. Maybe a beach honeymoon where she could finally put her feet up after years of sweat, grime and manual labor. But then what? Do you think her children scampered sweetly and sat at her feet when she sang, just as the birds and the mice did? Did she and the handsome prince argue about the latest frock she purchased at the town market? Was she now doing manual labor inside the castle, cooking and cleaning for a family of her own? When was it, the exact moment when she realized (as we all do) that love is not a fairy tale?

I had no idea what I was about to get into when I met my husband Miguel. I had been married before and knew very well that marriage requires daily dedication, nurturing, humility, and a steadfast strength when times get tough. My first marriage didn't end because of lack of commitment or hard work. It was doomed before it even started because I was too young to understand there are different kinds of love. My first husband was a good man and a wonderful father. I just didn't have the feelings a wife should have for her spouse. We worked on our relationship daily, for 16 years, before deciding we both deserved to find true love, passionate love.

While married though, my first husband and I were dedicated to our union and worked diligently, to create an efficient and caring team. We raised toddlers, juggled work and sleep deprivation—as all new parents do. We shared bills, paid our mortgage, split the chores and the childcare duties. We worried about money, parenting decisions and staying connected to our families and friends. We picked up toys, did mountains of laundry, raked leaves in the yard and cooked dinner. I even found time to leave little notes for my husband, to bring him a coffee at work and thank him, often, for the contributions he made to our little family. He did the same for me.

Yes, I knew about the work, but I didn't mind. I considered my first marriage to be an easy one. My husband and I never fought. Like never! I'm not lying. Our daily conversation was calm and polite. He agreed with absolutely everything I said. If I exclaimed the sky was green, he would comment on it's lovely hue. That was part of the problem, though. He agreed with absolutely everything I said. It leaves very little room for stimulating conversation. In retrospect, I can readily admit I am a strongly-opinionated person. I was very much in charge of running our household, parenting our children and organizing our social calendar. In truth, it was likely much easier to agree with me than to raise an objection. Perhaps my first husband's passive nature was a defense mechanism, or pure wisdom, or both.

Maybe some of you are shaking your heads wondering why I would have left such a lovely man. I often shook my own head, wondering why I didn't love him. He was an easy man to be married to, but I found it boring. My boredom turned into numbness and my numbness turned into depression. I craved a partner who would offer opinions, who would counter my thoughts and force me to grow. Our marriage was vanilla ice cream: a dependable, nice dessert but it was predictable. I wanted a little cayenne pepper sprinkled on top, some heat to spice things up. This love was easy, but it didn't fit me right. In fact, it felt all wrong.

In moments of brutal honesty, I would share my concerns with my husband. I figured he deserved to know how I felt.

"I feel as if we are just roommates," I explained, "I feel like there should be more than this. I want passion. I want excitement. I want love."

My husband would pat my hand with a lot of patience and a little condescension. "That kind of love isn't real, Kel. That love is in fairy tales. You watch too many movies. You read too many books. There are no fireworks and butterflies. It's fiction. This is reality, Kel. This is what love feels like."

I wasn't sure, but I had never been with another man, so I had no other love to compare this too. I had met my husband when I was 14 years old and began dating him at 16. He was all I knew. I chose to trust him instead of trusting myself.

An expert in emotional repression, I had no troubles pushing down my doubt. But like a French Press coffee, when you push down hard enough, liquid comes rushing to the top. It was a little routine I developed with my doubt. Push it down. Fine for a while. Then it rushes to the top. Repeat. It went on for years, until one day, the coffee press overflowed.

The little voice which started as a whisper, finally began to yell. "Pay attention to me!" it cried. "You are only 32 years old. Do you really want to live like this, stay wondering and unsure, for the next 60 years? Can you live your whole life and never explore the possibility of love?"

I couldn't.

So, divorce. Yada yada. Fear. Yada yada. Aloneness. Yada yada. So alone. Yada yada. Resurrection. Yada yada. Dating. Yada yada. Miguel.

Miguel is no vanilla ice cream. He is so spicy, it sometimes burns a little, leaving me to ponder, "What the hell was I thinking?" Miguel is exactly what I asked The Universe to send me. He is tall, dark and handsome, and I was attracted to his strong sense of masculinity. He is a romantic at heart, a man who holds doors open for women and whispers sexy Spanish into my ear. He calls me, "La Reina", or queen, and is confident enough to respect the woman I am, strong and independent. However, while he has a certain reverence for La Reina, he does not kneel to her. This man is about as opinionated as they come. In fairness, while his ideas are strong, he is willing to hear my thoughts, but will not agree unless I convince him. At times, it makes for fascinating conversation, verbal sparring which challenges beliefs and causes us to really examine our own ideas, while exploring other perspectives. Other times, it feels more like two bull-headed lawyers, arguing sides in a courtroom. And on many occasions, it's like two gladiators, matted with blood and sweat, battling to the death.

Yes, The Universe gave me exactly what I asked for and then sat back and laughed because I didn't know how to handle it.

Our relationship followed the path most new couples travel. The first year was absolute bliss. We were completely infatuated with each other, delirious we had found someone to love with such abandon. Did I say love? I meant lust. Because, let's be honest. In the first year of a relationship, however committed a couple may be, most of us are still on our best behavior. While Miguel and I spent copious hours in each other's apartments and packed many an overnight bag, the boundaries were still obvious. This was my space and that was his. When I stayed with him, I was a guest. He made my coffee, I cooked him dinner, and we both picked our dirty laundry off the floor— literally and figuratively. We spent our evenings strolling underneath the twinkle of city lights and spent our mornings lazily wrapped in each other's arms. Then, we would each go our separate ways, back to real life. Back to kids, to work, to ex-spouses and obligations. There was a very clear line drawn between the fantasy bubble in which we enjoyed each other's company and our day-to-day responsibilities.

I am so grateful for the first year of our courtship. It was what I had waited my whole adult life for, romantic kisses, candlelit dinners, exciting weekends away. It was passion and spice and fire like I had never known. It was fireworks and butterflies. What I was too naïve to understand, in those first glorious months, is that with passion, comes hatred. Life enjoys a balance, doesn't it? Before Miguel, I had never understood that love could be so closely tied with fury. It scared me.

Once Miguel and I moved in together, our emotions began to come in waves, loving and hating each other with equal intensity. It was a constant roller coaster of complete joy, followed by a plummet into despair, then passionate reconnection once again. We rarely agreed on anything and it was incredibly frustrating. We would battle about money, about parenting, about how much salt to use in our cooking. No topic, big or small, was off-limits. While in the beginning of our relationship we found our different perspectives interesting and refreshing, as we settled into day-to-day life together, it became exhausting. He was an alpha dog, used to having his own way and so was I. It was a recipe for disaster. The number of nights my girlfriends had to listen to me crying about the drama in my life is embarrassing. The number of times I questioned why I was putting up with this insanity is too high to tally. The number of times one of us had threatened to leave is more than I can remember. Yet, we are still together.

I believe love is forged in the dark times. It's easy to be with someone when everything is fireworks and butterflies. Resilience is built upon challenge. There is strength in choosing to stay, to grow, to become better. I wish I could tell you things became simpler in my marriage to Miguel. I can't. Each and every day, I choose to be with him, even though it's hard and it's infuriating. After seven years together, we are still working on our communication and learning to compromise. We still need to remind ourselves to pick our battles or to listen with an empathetic ear. Love isn't meant to be easy. It's meant to make us grow. Sharing your life with someone forces you to become a better person. And, I mean *forces*. Growth is uncomfortable! It can be ugly, graceless and messy, but—if you are willing to have patience, forgiveness and faith—standing strong through the hard times will reap the biggest rewards.

Couples in today's western society, so often give up without a fight. You may be thinking to yourself, "Hey Divorced Lady! Who are you to criticize the culture of failed marriages? Hypocritical!"

Yep, you got me. You may be right, however, I encourage you to read on for several reasons.

1. I was with my first husband for 16 years and I like to think I tried everything in my power to make it work before finally admitting it wasn't meant to be.

2. Being a divorced woman and experiencing the carnage of a broken marriage has taught me a thing or two. I like to think it has made me wiser when walking into a new relationship.

3. I am not judging anyone or any marriage. I am simply sharing some of the lessons I have learned the hard way in hopes it may ease someone else's pain. Take it or leave it, as you choose.

I'd like to tell you the story of the past 12 months of my marriage. I have already painted a picture, with broad strokes. Now, let me fill in the detail, so you may have a deeper understanding of my point: When life gets difficult, it's fear which voices the words of doubt. It's fear whispering things *shouldn't be this hard. Love shouldn't cause so much pain.* What I have learned, after walking through one of the most challenging seasons of our marriage, is the choice to weather the storm together will most definitely make a couple's relationship stronger.

A little over a year and a half ago, Miguel and I were enjoying a relatively blissful moment in our relationship. After years of busy pace, parenting and working, I was on a partial leave from my job as a teacher, while completing my Master's Degree. For the first time in my adult life, my pace was slow. Life was calm. I studied during the day, while my children were at school, and greeted them with cookies and smiles when they arrived home. When Miguel came home from work, each night, I was happy and fulfilled. I felt like a good mother and a good wife and we were happy.

Then, one day, he called me, an hour or so after arriving at work. "Good morning, mi amor. How are you?" I asked.

"I've been fired. I'm coming home."

I thought he was joking. Mere weeks before, the company he had worked at for 10 years had offered him a new position, a promotion of sorts. He was feeling successful and thriving in this new opportunity. Neither of us saw this coming. It seems the company was experiencing "corporate restructuring", which rendered Miguel's new position irrelevant to their future direction. The rug had been pulled out from under us.

While studying at university, I was only working two days per week. Initially, when Miguel lost his job, I wasn't worried, for the silver lining was that his company had offered him a small severance package. Financially, we would be fine for a few months. Emotionally, though, Miguel's ego had taken a hit. Once the shock of the news wore off, he fell into a rut of self-doubt and anger. Days went by and he wouldn't shower or leave the house without reminder. He stopped working out and spent hour after hour on the couch. The vivacious man I knew was slowly being sucked into a dark cloud of despair. This lasted for weeks. I missed my husband but remained patient and faithful that he would find his way out of the fog. I went about my days, reminding Miguel I loved him, but focused on my own happiness and generally tried to stay out of his way.

Despite his grouchiness and my concern for his well-being, we tried to find a bright side to the situation. In the entirety of our relationship, the two of us had rarely been home together. While working, Miguel used to leave the house at 5:30am and return at 7pm, just in time for dinner and a glass of wine before we went to bed. With both of us being off work, we were excited by the prospect of this unexpected blessing. We could go for lunch in the middle of the day! Sleep in and enjoy coffee in bed! We could make love at two o'clock in the afternoon! It was truly amazing! For a week or two. Then, the alpha dogs began to butt heads. Now that Miguel was home, he was suddenly very curious about how I spent my time. He had opinions about the groceries I chose to order and the stores at which I chose to buy them. He had thoughts about what I was going to cook for dinner and the brand of cleaner I used to tidy our house. Some days, I clamped my lips together, fearful of the words that may come spewing out of my mouth. Other days, I was not as successful in my attempts to use self-restraint. We began to fight. A lot.

In the midst of this battlefield, after a few weeks of contemplation, Miguel decided he loved being home. He had time to enjoy hobbies he hadn't dabbled in for years. He could watch soccer on TV in the middle of the day! He could read and go for long runs! He could beat on his drum kit and rock out on the electric guitar! Maybe being fired was the best thing that had ever happened to him! His new ambition became finding a job which allowed him to stay at home, permanently. Several months into his "work vacation", he informed me of his intention to invest in the stock market and become a professional trader. It would, he explained, take him a year or so to master and, therefore, he would not be returning to work any time soon. This new venture would require all of his focus. Excuse me, WHAT?!

Now, I am a champion of personal evolution. I believe in taking risks and chasing your dreams. However, those dreams are usually sought after as a side hustle until they become a more dependable and consistent source of income, for the mortgage still needs to be paid. What a buzzkill! My husband's declaration that he intended to take a year off terrified me. He is incredibly savvy with money and would never put us at risk of financial ruin, however, the thought of cutting back to the bare minimum of financial existence was incredibly uncomfortable. For me. He was confident everything would be just fine. In hindsight, he was right, but I didn't see it at the time. Fear clouded my vision.

I tried to be a supportive wife, despite my doubts and fears. I wouldn't be the person who squashed his dreams, and that became my mantra. When he looked back on this time, I wanted him to have gratitude for my support and not resent me for holding him back. I was willing to sacrifice in order to keep the status quo. *No more lattes? No problem. No more restaurants? That's okay. No new shoes? I can handle it.* However, I drew the line when it came to my kids. They didn't sign up for this. Somehow, I still needed to pay for their field trips and after school activities, so I set out to find some side gigs, determined to fill the financial gap we found ourselves in.

The year before, I had written a parenting book and felt the logical thing was to organize some speaking engagements. I was happy to spend my evenings with a group of teachers or parents, discussing my passion for raising resilient children. I also stumbled across a teaching position at the university where I was doing my Master's Degree and was pleased to discover that teaching adults was a rewarding and thought-provoking experience. Within a few weeks, the relaxing pace of life I had been enjoying vanished. My days were now spent either teaching at the elementary school or conducting research and writing papers to further my own education. My nights were filled with speaking engagements or commuting to the university to take classes or teach courses for the undergraduates. I was also working on a new book and would wake up in the wee hours of the morning to get some writing done before the chaos of the day ensued. On top of my work obligations, I was still a wife and a mother, cooking dinners, folding laundry and chauffeuring to soccer practice.

Truth be told, I became envious of Miguel's leisurely lifestyle. Envy slowly festered until it became resentment. I wish I could tell you I was a better person, that I was happy for him. But I wasn't. I was emotionally and physically exhausted. To be clear, I don't blame Miguel for my hectic schedule. He never asked me to pick up the slack. On the contrary, he kept insisting I didn't need to. However, a workaholic by nature, driven by my own ambitious dreams and the carnal need to care for my family, I barged full steam ahead for months, existing on very little sleep and trying my damnedest to be everything for everyone.

I was, in fact, driven by fear. Fear can be an excellent motivator. Fear of missing out is what makes us work hard, grasping at opportunities and inspiring us to keep going. I was afraid my children would miss out on parties, sports, field trips and other childhood experiences, due to our financial constraints. I also felt certain my career was about to take off and was scared that if I didn't say yes to every single request, this window of opportunity would pass and another one would not surface in its wake. After all, I'm no spring chicken and chasing a new career at 40 put me in the late bloomer category. Yes, fear can be motivating, but when it causes us to create an imbalance in our lives, it can become detrimental. I was burning the candle at both ends, and one can only sustain that pace for so long. The irony of it all was, despite my burgeoning success—or perhaps because of it—I feared my family was suffering due to my long hours. I simply was not as available as they were used to. Guilt. The straw that broke my back.

My stress began as a stomach ache that wouldn't go away. Then it morphed into days in which I was so exhausted, I couldn't get out of bed. It escalated into panic attacks in the middle of the night. I ignored it all, determined not to let these weaknesses get the best of me. The load was becoming heavier—crushing really—but I marched on. My denial, though, was getting the best of my marriage.

We stopped having sex. Using every ounce of energy just to exist through the course of my day left me with nothing to offer my husband once our heads hit the pillow. Miguel and I have always said that sex is what has held us together in the tough times. Even in our lowest moments, sex is what allowed us to break the tension, dissolve the anger and dissipate the hopelessness. It had been what rekindled the passion and rebuilt the bridge of connection between us. Now, that lifeline was gone and I was a ship drifting at sea.

As I sunk slowly into depression, Miguel stood by, helpless, distraught at his inability to save me. At one point, I cried for nearly 60 days straight. When I say "cried", I mean sobbed. Each and every day. Some days, out of guilt. Others, out of frustration. Others still, I had no freaking clue why I was crying. Miguel quietly wiped my tears and held me. At this point, when I was at my lowest and my most vulnerable, fear crept into my brain and told me that love should be easy. Life should be enjoyable. If I wasn't happy, something must be wrong. A logical person would have analyzed the situation and remembered the history of depressive episodes which had plagued me in the past. They tend to manifest in seasons where I am overworked and overwhelmed. Considering this, my current depression was not all that surprising. However, fear is not logical. It is a bold-faced liar. Fear told me my exhaustion was the result of a marriage that had always been hard work. So I, the woman who had spent the last two years researching resilience, decided the best course of action would be to quit my marriage. I was desperately unhappy and figured the best way to save my mental health would be to take a break from my relationship.

Heartbroken, Miguel could do nothing as he watched me pack a bag to leave. The only thing he asked was that I take some time to decide if splitting up was what I truly wanted. He gently suggested it could be the depression talking and was worried I was making a decision I would regret in the future. "If you begin to feel better and you still want to leave me, then we'll discuss it."

My parents' house was vacant for the summer, so I set up camp in their home and counted my blessings that I had a safe place to stay. My children were with their father, shielded from the mess of my depression and marriage drama. There I stayed for two months. Each day, I simply focused on maintaining my mental health. I went to counselling. I did yoga, meditated, and went on long runs. I wrote, read books, and went to bed early. I would speak to Miguel once a day, simply to let him know I was alright.

Depression is terrifying, for it feels as if your brain is betraying you. At least, that's how it feels to me. I had watched Miguel battle his demons earlier in the year. Some days, a different set of eyes stared back at me. The soft, brown eyes I knew were replaced by a vacant pair, no love within them. Now I was deep in the trenches myself. My feelings had vacated my body, leaving behind an empty shell of a person. My normal Type A personality, driven by productivity and joy, was replaced by a lifeless form who could barely function. I had to remind myself to eat and to call my children. My inner voice, which has always reminded me to look for the life lesson, to handle adversity with grace, to grab the bull by the horns and go for it, receded and was replaced by something sinister. This new voice told me to save my family from the misery I caused. It compelled me to remove myself and let them thrive in my absence. In the moments when the voice became quiet, all that remained was numbness. No joy. No fear. No feelings whatsoever. This can be scary, in and of itself.

After weeks of intensive self-care, I slowly began to feel more like myself. There would be glimpses of my old self, moments when I could feel calm, or appreciation, or a lightness. I began to reach out to Miguel. The poor man had waited in relationship purgatory for the entire summer. Our marriage was essentially broken, torn down to the studs. Now it was time to decide if it could be saved. We had a choice to make: we could walk away and begin new lives, or we could commit to putting in the necessary work, re-building our relationship to be better, stronger. We still loved each other, but needed to see if the damage was repairable. Tentatively, Miguel and I began to date. Every few days, we would meet for a walk or to grab a cup of coffee. The conversation was awkward and cautious, Miguel careful not to get his hopes up or to trigger an emotional response from me. At each of our dates, the internal battle within me was exhausting, as I fought to quiet the voice of depression, so I could form a connection with the man I loved so much. Sometimes, the connection lasted for a few minutes, sometimes only for a second before the numbness would set in again. Miguel was incredibly patient. He could see through the struggle and trusted my desire to come back to him. Even though the dates were painful for both of us, we persevered and kept coming back for more. Slowly, it became easier to be together and we knew our love would conquer this.

Eventually, I moved back into our home. The first few months felt cautious, for Miguel was constantly searching for signs I would break once again. Fear whispered in my ear. *He may not forgive you for walking out on him.* But this time, I was smart enough to tell fear to shove it. I worked hard to earn Miguel's trust, to slow my pace and take care of myself. Over time, we returned to a new sense of normal, one based on honest and open communication. We've since had countless conversations about stress, overscheduling, depression and anxiety. It's a constant dialogue and something we choose to work on every day, even when we don't want to.

I will be forever grateful that Miguel was wise enough to wait out my depression. He had faith in us, even when I didn't. He knew that love is not meant to be easy and he stood strong when I couldn't.

What the Warrior Says:

LESSON 1:
MARRIAGE IS HARD! IF IT ISN'T, PERHAPS YOU AREN'T ALL THAT INVESTED.

"What's NOT hard? That's the question you should be asking. It's an easier one to answer. Yes, marriage is hard! Parenting is hard. Relationships are hard. Being a grown-ass woman is hard. Do you know why it's hard? It's hard because you care deeply and so you should. It's hard because The Universe wants you to grow. It's providing opportunities for you to evolve, to see things from a

*different perspective, to be stronger and gentler at the same time.
Hard is not a bad thing. It means you're on the right track."*

The thing is, none of us sign up for this. I didn't sign up for
Miguel losing his job and the gloomy weeks that followed. He
most certainly didn't sign up for a wife who struggles with her
mental health. Love is hard. Love is a choice. Almost every
day, I see posts on Facebook where people are smiling with
their spouse and the caption reads, "My favorite human!" or
some variation of that statement. It's truly lovely. However,
it's easy to spend time together when life is fun and stress-
free. True love, deep love, comes from standing by that person
when they are your *least* favorite human.

For many reasons, my marriage is not easy. Along with
financial tight spots and blips in our mental health, we have
to slog through raising a blended family, cultural and language
differences, conflicting opinions, ex-spouses and, and, and …
The list is long. I'm sure your list is long as well. Everyone
comes with their own set of issues and no relationship is
perfect. You can either look at the list as a reason to pack up
and get the hell outta dodge, or you can accept the list as the
reason you are growing into a stronger, wiser, more empathetic
person. As difficult as the last year has been, I am grateful for
it. I am living my life more mindfully and investing in my
marriage with more intention than I ever had before. They
say, what doesn't kill you makes you stronger. If that's not true
about love, I don't know what is.

My marriage to my first husband was a walk in the park on a
spring day. It didn't cause me pain or despair but that's because

I wasn't emotionally invested in it. I liked my life, but never cultivated an intimate emotional connection with my spouse. When you become emotionally tied to another human, that's where the magic happens. That's also where the hurt lives. They say the people we love the most are also the people who hurt us the most. We hurt them too. We care so much for their well-being, their opinions matter, and our lives would be less colorful without them. It's scary, knowing someone has the power to hurt you that deeply so choosing to be with them involves a terrifying level of trust. When the day inevitably comes, when you hurt each other, it's fear who screams, "*I told you so! Don't let this happen again!*"

But if you can recognize the voice of fear, and counter it with the voice of grace, your relationship will undoubtedly grow within difficult moments. I read somewhere, the definition of "grace" is forgiving someone, even when they don't necessarily deserve it. There have been many moments in my marriage to Miguel when one or both of us did not deserve forgiveness. In those moments, I try to remind myself to look at the big picture. Will this matter in a year? In a decade? Do I want to be with this man in a year? In a decade? Will he want to be with me if I continue down the path I'm on?

A healthy marriage cannot rest on a foundation of fear, even if there is an abundance of love. Solid marriages are based on the pillars of humility, grace, resilience, and faith. Being married to Miguel is one of the most challenging choices I've ever made. It's also one of the choices I am most proud of.

At some point in the course of every day, Miguel and I will look each other in the eyes and whisper, "Today, I choose to marry you." Marriage and love are not static, one-time choices. They are verbs and require daily action and attention. Some days, the act of marriage and love is simple, inspired by affection and connection. I choose to put toothpaste on your toothbrush in the morning. You choose to make my coffee. However, those choices become increasingly important in times of adversity. Even in the moment when I can't stand to be around Miguel and he finds me repulsive, we still say, "Today, I choose to marry you." I didn't put toothpaste on your freaking toothbrush, but dammit, I'm still here. I'm not going anywhere. For in the midst of hate, we acknowledge the choice to stay, to honor our commitment and to grow.

LOVE SHOULD BE EASY

"Hard is not a bad thing. It means you're on the right track."

1. How do you want to show up each day for your spouse?

2. What is preventing this from being your reality?

3. Are there any emotions or stories you need to let go of when it comes to love and what you deserve?

4. If you could show up, in an ideal way, how would it change your relationship?

Chapter 4

FEAR SAYS:

"THIS IS NOT WHAT A FAMILY LOOKS LIKE"

My parents have been married for 43 years. I'm sure it hasn't always been easy. In fact, I know it hasn't. However, they still truly enjoy each other's company. It's very cute. They set off in their little convertible sports car, top down, golf clubs in the back. They hike, travel, go on bike rides or enjoy a glass of wine and a book. They have modelled a respectful, dedicated union for almost half a century. It's remarkable.

Despite this shining example of love and commitment, my sister and I are both divorced. My brother has never married. How could this possibly be? (I am sure my parents have lamented this very question on more than one occasion.) Was it fear of missing out on something better? Something easier? Something more romantic and exciting? Fear of hard work and commitment? Even with the best role models one could ask for, my siblings and I have either a) dared not venture down this road or b) tried this marriage thing and crashed and burned miserably the first time around.

I won't dare speak for my siblings. (They would hunt me down, pin me down and pinch me all over.) But I will say, personally, I view the dissolution of my first marriage as a colossal failure, even though it was absolutely necessary and I don't regret it. Despite the faith I had in the decision I was making, we are talking about the Queen Overachiever, here. The one who fears failure more than vampires fear garlic and the Real Housewives fear a Botox shortage. Failure was not an option in anything I pursued. Yet, I messed up the biggest, most-valued goal I had in life—to create the perfect family.

I won't bore you with the sordid details of my divorce. (Although you may read about it in a fabulous little book called *Ridiculous, Resilient Me*. Seriously, I think you should buy it.) Long story short, despite the fact my first husband was (and is) a good man, I wasn't in love with him. I met and married him at a very young age, before I understood that life brings us different kinds of love: platonic, familial, and lusty. Unfortunately, this person, my husband, fell into the platonic category. It was heartbreaking for both of us when I realized I couldn't spend my entire adult life without knowing romantic love.

When I left my husband, I wasn't scared of being single. I had bigger fish to fry! At that point, I feared …

1. The psychological damage I had done to my children. Would they forgive me for causing all of this sadness and destroying the safety and security of their world? Have I forever tainted their view on marriage?

2. What people would think of me, the woman who destroyed her family. Would I lose the support of friends I have had for decades? Are people judging me, casting me aside as a selfish homewrecker?

3. I wouldn't be able to pay the mortgage. Would my children be subjected to poverty, bare cupboards, and grumbling tummies? Am I destined to work two or three jobs to cover the cost of my bills?

No, being single was the least of my concerns. In fact, I knew I had no business dating anyone until I got my life in order and learned how to stand strong on my own.

All fears aside, I had faith in myself. I knew I was smart and hard-working. The weighty pit in my stomach was very motivating. I refused to let my actions affect my children and I was determined to provide them with the best life I could. I would work hard to heal my pain so I could be the mother they deserved to have. For as long as it took to return their sense of safety, I would soothe my children, reassure them they were loved. I would work as many hours as needed to provide them with a secure home. My innate "I've got this" drive-to-survive kicked into high gear.

I also knew if I paid attention to my lengthy list of fears, it would cripple me, rendering me paralyzed and useless. I desperately needed to reframe my fear in a way that gave me back my power. I stopped using the words "selfish", "homewrecker" and "destroyer", deciding to cast aside all negativity and choosing, instead, to see strength in what I had done. I had faced my greatest fear—failing my family—and made the most difficult choice in my life because I knew it was the right one. If I teach my children anything in life, I hope they always follow their gut, no matter how illogical, scary or unknown that path may be. Never let fear hold you back from living your truth.

I also knew I was modelling marriage and love for my boys. Children are always watching us, trying to make sense of the world and what it means to be an adult. Though we can't control their perception of the actions they see, the feelings they feel and the words they hear, we can do our very best to be mindful of the powerful role parents play. We show them how people should treat us and how we should treat others. We demonstrate the desire to go after their dreams or shrink from them. We model the standards we adhere to. Would I want my children to stay in a relationship that their hearts weren't in? Would I want *my* marriage for my children? No. I want them to chase love. I want them to have fireworks and butterflies and all the emotions that come with falling head over heels. I want them to know passion and dedication and meaningful connection. How could I possibly teach this to them if I wasn't willing to go for it myself?

I heard a beautiful quote by author, Glennon Doyle, in a podcast the other day. I wish I had known it 10 years ago when I left my husband. Though I can't magically bestow this wisdom on my younger self, I *can* share it with you. Maybe someone out there needs to hear it today.

Doyle said, "My children don't need me to save them. They need to watch me save myself."

That's precisely what I was doing all those years ago. I was saving myself. Saving myself from the numbness, which had settled in as a defense mechanism, allowing me to exist within a marriage I knew in my heart was wrong. Saving myself from the self-hatred which was brewing as a result of my refusal to make the hard choice. Saving myself from a life lived in monotones of grey, in the absence of true love and desire.

Since that time, there have been many instances in my life when I have had to hurt others or disappoint them in order to save my own soul. I will share some of these stories with you. This selfishness doesn't make me a bad person. It makes me real and brave and wise. Maybe it's not selfishness at all. Maybe it's simply the pursuit of integrity, an acknowledgement of my deep longing to have the girl inside me live the life she is meant for. Maybe it's a desire to have my insides and my outsides match. Maybe.

As I focused on rebuilding my life as a single mother of two young children, my boys and I had many bedtime conversations about family. That's when children seem to express their inner most wonderings, isn't it? As the daylight fades away and parents tuck them safely into bed and kiss their foreheads, big questions emerge. Will you and Daddy get back together? Do you still love him? Will you love someone else? Are we still a family?

Are we still a family? … My definition of family had always been a traditional one. Father, mother, children. That's what I had growing up, what was modeled for me. Are we still a family? My children, in their grief and innocence, had hit upon my own fear, a fear I wasn't ready to examine. In my own wondering of that question, the pain of this particular nerve was still raw and unbearable. Yet, my children deserved to have this conversation and I had an inkling they held more wisdom than I did.

"What is a family, my loves?" I asked my boys.

"A family is a group of people who love each other," they decided. We loved each other more than anything in the world, so, yes, we were still a family, one that looked very different than anything I had ever known or expected. As I reassured my children and redefined their version of family, I simultaneously had to make peace with that idea myself.

Okay, back to my love life, because I know you may be wondering. We left off with my decision that I wouldn't fear being alone. I decided I would accept whatever fate The Universe would hand out. Maybe, one day, I would be blessed with a gorgeous, rich and generous second husband. We would spend our days travelling the world on a private jet, drinking in sophistication and culture, with a martini in hand. Or, I would become an old, wrinkly spinster with cobwebs collecting in my lady parts. I would need to be content with my family, friends and hobbies, living a fulfilling life without the company of a man. As I came to terms with this possible outcome, I swore on my life I would NEVER be the spinster who owned multiple cats. That's not accepting your fate. That's succumbing to it. Truth be told, I mentally prepared for both options and I was crossing my fingers for the first, but felt I may deserve the second.

Luckily karma blessed me with something in between. Though sadly not ridiculously wealthy (there are no helicopters and vineyards in my present marriage), my new beau was very handsome and charming. And he came with a plus one—his son.

Here's the straight talk. Blending families is literally the most challenging thing I have ever done. Harder than giving birth (excruciating but short-term pain). Harder than choosing divorce (devastating, but with an eye toward a better future). Harder than parenting teenagers (hair-pulling years, but equally rewarding). Honestly, I had no idea what I was signing up for. I entered this union with all the wisdom of a sweet baby lamb skipping toward the slaughter house, excited for a mysterious adventure. My little-lamb brain was full of naivety. My intention was that Miguel and I would bring our exes into the fold of our new life and the four of us would parent with grace and respect, always keeping the children's best interests at the forefront. I envisioned all of us as friends. We would invite our exes and their new spouses for Sunday afternoon BBQs, where all the children would play while we laughed and swapped stories. Butterflies would spread their glittery wings in the sun. Unicorns would gallop and swish their rainbow hair and little leprechauns would dance the Macarena. While it may not be surprising to you, the fact our exes didn't want to participate in my utopian vision was shocking to me. I guess it's one thing to come to terms with the dissolution of a marriage. It's quite another to see your ex finding happiness with someone else. That reality is harder to accept with grace.

My precious baby-lamb brain also assumed our new family unit would blend harmoniously. Between us, Miguel and I had 3 wonderful boys who shared a lot in common. They were close in age. They all loved sports and music. It made sense to me they would get along seamlessly and our house would be filled with laughter and love. Wrong again. While the boys were happy getting to know a new playmate, they did not always enjoy the dynamics of another adult in the house, especially one who grabbed the attention of their parent. Being parented by your father's new wife or your mother's new husband was a strange new phenomenon—one which our boys found uncomfortable. There were many questions asked and we definitely experienced some push back as all five of us worked through our growing pains. The boys fought to establish a pecking order amongst themselves. Collective groans were heard as we established new boundaries and agreed upon rules and expectations for behavior. Things were changing for all of us and, at times, it wasn't fun. However, despite a rocky start, a new normal emerged as time passed and relationships were established. In truth, though, our children accepted this blended family with more ease than both Miguel and I.

Allowing someone else to parent your child is hard as hell. It requires a level of trust not many can cultivate. It hurts your heart when consequences are imposed by another. It takes every ounce of will and strength not to step in and intervene— even when the discipline is fair and just—especially, when the child involved looks at you with crocodile tears dripping down their cheeks.

The funny dynamic of stepparenting, (I say "funny" but I mean "complex, complicated, humbling") is this—you can care for another's child, feed them, console them, play with them and chauffeur them, but at the end of the day, that child does not belong to you. That's the hard truth. Their biological parents always have executive-decision-making powers, regardless of your advice or opinion. Even though you try to maintain a team approach to parenting, there will be times when you just aren't a team due to the unequal balance of power.

In the first year of our marriage, my happy bubble of naivety violently burst. I began to fear that what I created wasn't truly a family. My children and I had decided, years ago, that a family was a group of people who loved each other. While there was love in my house, there was also a tremendous amount of uncertainty, discomfort and even resentment. There was so much unanticipated separation between us. You go this way. We'll go that way. I didn't know how to define our unit, as it didn't fit into the traditional definition of family I had grown up with—or even definition 2.0.

As our children navigated two separate worlds—our home and the home of their other biological parent—they were often forced to juggle varying expectations, rules, and experiences. A child's capacity to adapt to their surroundings often blows me away. While it often took a day or two to adjust (and they occasionally needed reminders of the expectations at our home), all three boys went back and forth with grace and resilience. That is not to say it was easy for any of us. Adding to the complexity of this new dynamic was my own guilt. A mother's heart holds a special place for guilt, doesn't it? I began to fear I would never be able to offer our children a traditional family home.

Ironically, while I framed our family in the most positive way for my little humans, I didn't believe my own sentiments. I would exclaim, "How lucky you are to have so many people who love you!" "You have bonus parents! That's so cool!" "I wish I had 2 Christmases and 2 birthdays!" Inside, I would marinate in the fear that my boys would be affected by the stress and frustration that inevitably happens when dealing with a new marriage, blended family and ex-spouses. *This is not what a family looks like*, said Fear.

Miguel and I don't always see eye to eye when it comes to parenting. I think this may be typical of all parenting relationships, however, there is one major difference in a blended family. Ultimately, I am responsible for my children and he is responsible for his. I wish I could tell you we always worked to find a common ground and a compromise we were both comfortable with. In the early days of our marriage, finding a common ground wasn't always possible and we often found ourselves in situations when our children had to abide by different rules. It was hard not to become resentful and although we knew we were failing, Miguel and I didn't know what else to do.

We began to avoid any situation that may cause us to argue. Our marriage was still new, a marital fetus of sorts, vulnerable and not yet fully developed. Wanting to protect our relationship and shelter our children from toxicity, we often chose to operate as separate entities when the family was together. I would take my children to the beach and he would stay home with this son. They would go skiing and we would go to the movies. Both Miguel and I truly desired to be a cohesive family unit, but it was just too hard. Every time we were all together, our stress and anxiety made the experience unenjoyable. The kids loved it. But Miguel and I were giant stress-balls. We would plaster fake smiles on our faces and mentally create lists of annoyances to argue about later, behind closed doors. Thus, avoidance became the lesser of two evils. We even began to vacation separately.

Miguel and I had both committed to our marriage with the hope of establishing a family together. It turns out, the cookie-cutter version of family is not easily replicated. Our blended family was more complicated than either of us could have ever imagined. The failure to create a relaxed, cohesive unit of humans who loved each other hurt. It was a constant ache that never went away—like the pulsing of a phantom limb, or the sizzling of an angry burn. Realizing we may never be able to create a united family was like admitting to the death of a dream. And we mourned. For years, our emotions oscillated around blame, shame, anger, sadness, and defeat. Rather than focusing on creating a new vision for our family, we were stuck in the loss of what we weren't. We even struggled to use the word "family" when referring to our little unit. "Team" didn't seem appropriate either. "Wolf-pack" implied one strong leader, and we had two. "Grouping"? "Co-habitators"? The futile attempt to put a label on what we were was getting ridiculous!

Five years following the trauma of my divorce, the same question emerged, the same fear bubbled within me. "Are we a family?"

Some days, we could find a sliver of acceptance. Others, we tried to use humor to hide our true feelings. Avoidance remained our favourite tactic. Many days, Miguel and I became overwhelmed by our disappointment and it took a toll on our marriage. You see, avoidance causes disconnect and being disconnected from your spouse for days at a time is damaging. I can't tell you how many times one of us, or both of us, questioned if all of this hurt was worth it. Was our love strong enough to rise above one of life's great disappointments?

I turned to my mother for advice. She has always been the glue that held our complicated little family together and I so badly wanted to be that foundation for mine. Thinking my mom could offer some perspective, I was taken aback when she replied she had none to offer. She had never experienced a similar situation. While her heart broke for me, she had no wisdom to share. "I don't know what I would do, if I were you," she said.

You may remember that my parents have been married for centuries. They have honored the "until death do us part" commitment. As did their parents, as well as the majority of their siblings and friends. My mom simply had no experience from which to draw upon and impart some wise advice. With love and sympathy in her heart, she told me she couldn't relate to what I was going through. As much as she wanted to soothe me and guide me, she had never traveled this road, nor walked beside someone as they made this journey. This was unknown territory for both of us.

In that moment, I realized, within a single generation, society has blown apart the idea of a traditional family. Of course my mom could not relate to my situation! Her parents were married until death. My dad's parents were married for 50 years. All of their friends were married and the occasional divorce was swept under the rug as an embarrassing failure. In their generation, a family was composed of a man and a woman raising biological children. That's it. There were no other options. Single parenthood, second marriages and same-sex parents have only recently begun to be accepted by society. This open-minded definition of family seems so commonplace now, that I had forgotten it hasn't always been the norm.

So, I turned to my girlfriends for advice.

My girlfriends are a colorful bunch of women, with a wide range of personal, professional, and romantic experience. Some of them enjoy happy, stable marriages. Some are single parents, dating, and hoping to find a second chance at love.

Some have dimmed their active search for love, choosing instead to focus on themselves and their children. Some are enjoying the dating life but have no desire to engage in the depth and complications of a relationship. All of them, of course, had a multitude of thoughts to share on life, love and relationships. Most of my girls could empathize with the idea of rebuilding a life after divorce, with the enormity of love and worry as a parent and with the complex nature of being a stepparent. All of them reminded me I was a strong and intelligent woman, worthy of love. My happiness and the happiness of my children were of utmost importance. The only thing I needed to decide was how this happiness would look. Was it possible in this life I had chosen? Marriage is a choice, not an obligation. I can stand strong as a single woman and mother, or I could stand strong within my complicated marriage. This was my decision to make, not to be influenced by others. To my disappointment (although I knew they were right), none of my girlfriends told me what I should do. Some of them shared their experiences and all of them listened while I shared mine through laughter and tears. Even though I still did not have a solid conclusion for myself, I felt better simply being in the presence of people who understood. (All of this is not to negate the efforts of my sweet mother. Her wisdom is the eternal voice in my head and her support for whatever choices I make in life is what allows me to be strong and to take risks.)

I began to realize that within the uncertainty I was feeling, there was also a sense of power. For my generation, there are no rules in terms of what constitutes a "proper" family. With the lack of rules, there may also be a lack of judgment by others. In fact, this wide open space allows room for us to use our *better* judgment, to do what we know in our hearts is best, without fear of wearing the scarlet letter. Within one generation, society has redefined the notion of what a secular family is or should be. While this may have positive and negative connotations, both of which have been discussed, we are not confined by societal rules. This lack of expectation may bring confusion but also offers freedom. I don't judge you for the choices you make in regard to your own happiness. (Provided that what brings you happiness is safe and respectful for yourself and those around you.) I don't judge you for adopting babies as a single parent. I don't judge you for focusing on your children and keeping a fun and affectionate friend on the side. I don't judge you for staying in a marriage that is difficult. I don't judge you for sharing your home with someone while enjoying your own independent life. I don't judge you for focusing on yourself, your work and your friends and taking love off the table. And, I don't feel judged for navigating through my complicated life with an absence of grace.

What the Warrior Says:

LESSON 1:
FORGING UNKNOWN TERRITORIES DOESN'T NEED TO BE FEARFUL. IT CAN BE EMPOWERING.

"Screw what other people think! The only thing that matters is what you think. Everything is what you make of it. If you decide something is terrible, or it's not meant to be, that becomes a

self-fulfilling prophecy. If you decide your family is a failure, then it is. So decide better. Maybe it's time to let go of what you thought your life would be and begin appreciating it for what it is. Your mindset is a choice and it will make or break your reality."

Most of my fear and guilt regarding my family arose from pressuring myself to comply with someone else's rules, someone else's version of family. It's the age-old notion of a square peg in a round hole. Once Miguel and I accepted the reality that we would never fit the traditional version of family, we became free to explore our own version. We let go of all the things we aren't and began to talk about the things we *are*. We made peace with our losses and started to turn our minds and hearts toward the possibilities.

It was important to acknowledge the dreams we lost. For years, we tried to feign acceptance, sweep aside sorrow and hide frustration. Having read how I bury negative emotions, you can imagine how that played out. (Picture volcanoes erupting and geysers shooting into the air.) In moments when Miguel and I were calm and ready to stop casting blame, we were finally able to empathize with each other's sorrow and let go of our own pain. We would never have a family unit which was cohesive, connected and joyful all of the time. It was a large pill to swallow.

Let's be honest. Is any family cohesive, connected, and joyful all the time? Even families in the "traditional" sense have their struggles. Take my own family, for example. My sister and I fought and hissed like cats from the time she was born until we were adults. It is only in the last few years we have been able to find true appreciation for each other and our differences. My brother is a drug addict and I haven't spoken to him in years. The logical side of my brain can acknowledge each and every family on this planet is vastly and beautifully complicated. All families simultaneously hold love and pain. The emotional side of my brain, however, held tightly onto an idealized version of family, an unattainable and unrealistic standard that no one could ever possibly live up to.

My first marriage fit the typical definition of family: husband, wife, children—yet in that scenario, the wife didn't love the husband. Is that better or worse than the version of family I am currently trying to forge? I have to admit, even with the hurt, the bruised egos and the confusion, the life I am living now and the family we are evolving into is preferable to the former option, hands down.

Instead of giving you a long list of our troubles and our family struggles, I would like to provide a list of the things we *are* and the blessings we have, so you might be able to understand how much power there can be in reframing our thoughts.

- Our children get along well and enjoy each other's company. This, in and of itself, is a huge win.

- The different perspectives Miguel and I often have force us to be open-minded and expose us to new ideas. Our communication skills have improved enormously in the course of our marriage, as has our ability to empathize and set aside ego for a greater purpose.

- Sometimes, the five of us enjoy adventures together, yet we also respect the need to focus on our own children at times. The moments when we choose to roll separately do not make us less than or worse than other families. It makes us unique.

- Having a stepparent who is not as emotionally attached can be a blessing. They can offer calm and logical views in situations that may be stressful and confusing for the biological parent and child.

- While we may not always be connected in traditional ways, we have created an environment where everyone feels safe and secure.

- Miguel and I do not need to conform to other people's versions of family and marriage. As long as our children are happy and our version makes sense to us, screw what everyone else thinks!

In the past 10 years, my little family has broken and rebuilt itself more than once. Each time we rebuild, it is with a deeper understanding of love and acceptance. We don't need to conform or squeeze ourselves into a mold that doesn't fit us. We allow ourselves the space we need to grow into fuller versions of who we are and who we want to be, as individuals and as a unit. The process of this evolution hasn't been easy, but in working through our growing pains, I have been able to forgive my fears that we are not a family and find some peace in the complexity of our relationships. I have a hunch my family will continue to deconstruct and rebuild itself as the years march on. My children will mature and move out of my home. They will form their own relationships, their own versions of family. And, no matter what the future holds, we will all be okay. These boys will always have my heart and that is family enough for me.

LESSON 2:
BEING A STEPPARENT IS LIKE HAVING YOUR NAME AS A SUPPORTING ROLE ON THE MARQUEE.

"Our egos have the power to take us down, to ruin everything that is good and crush all potential. There is brilliance in knowing when to exercise humility. Even the strongest of warriors know when to recede."

As a mother, my name is on the marquee in enormous letters with shining lights. I am the center of my children's world, their protector, their guide, their safe place. As a stepparent, my name is in tiny letters, barely legible, underneath Miguel's name. And, that's okay.

In the early days of my marriage to Miguel, I wanted to play a starring role in his son's life. I wanted to be his protector, his guide and his safe place too, just as I was to my own children. Here's the problem with that. Neither Miguel, his son, nor his ex-wife wanted me to play that role. So I was setting myself up for failure. I needed to realize Miguel's son already had two loving parents who were working to raise him, despite their differences. My determination to be involved in an intricate manner was getting in the way and complicating an already-complex situation. While my intentions were good, my efforts only served to make everyone (including me) uncomfortable and resentful. My advice wasn't being heard because they didn't want my advice.

The realization that my ego was out of control broke this negative cycle. I desperately wanted Miguel's son to love visiting our home and to connect emotionally with me. When he didn't, it was a shock. I am a charming human being! I am fun. I am kind. I plan adventures and bake cupcakes. Why doesn't he like me?

When my ego finished its tantrum (which lasted years, by the way) I was able to step back, quiet my pride and look objectively at the situation. Of course Miguel's son has a complicated relationship with me. Logically, it makes complete sense. He didn't choose for his parents to dissolve their marriage. He felt torn between loyalty to his mother and the need to form an alliance with a new instant-family. His hesitation to join the folds of our family wasn't about me, yet I took it personally.

As a parenting consultant, resilience researcher, and educator, I often offer professional advice on helping children overcome adversity. In my work life, my advice is sought-after and parents are usually grateful for my support. This was not the case in my own home, however. I had to learn—the hard way—that unsolicited advice is usually unwelcome. As helpful as I believe my experience may be, I have no right to impose it upon Miguel and his ex-wife. When they didn't ask for my advice, my ego was bruised. I was making the situation about me, not about them. If they were working together, making choices they felt were best for their son, who was I to intervene? This complicated sharing of perspective went both ways, as Miguel would often offer his thoughts on my parenting, only to have me reject his opinions.

Talking about someone's parenting is a sensitive topic, especially when there are varying opinions. In truth, Miguel and I still don't do well with these discussions. What we have learned, however, is to tread lightly. We will begin by asking if the other would like to hear our thoughts, and if they decline, that must be respected. If we decide we are brave enough to engage in that conversation, it must be done with the greatest empathy, all judgment reserved. We speak in observations and offer suggestions, understanding those thoughts may or may not be agreed with. These conversations are hard to have with grace, especially when you are on the receiving end of the advice but it's not impossible.

My greatest lesson in all of our struggles to stepparent with humility is this—my job is not to have a starring role in Miguel's son's life. I am a minor player, albeit an important one. My role is to support Miguel in the most challenging job he will ever have—to be a good parent. I will be his sounding board, his teammate, his safe place to express his fears. I will offer advice when asked for, will zip my lips when my advice is unwanted and will not react when my opinion is unheard. I will help him correct his mistakes, when they inevitably happen. I will create a safe, loving space in which his son feels like he belongs. I will encourage Miguel to bond with his child, whether that be in the company of me and my children or in the context of their own separate adventures.

Pushing ego aside and accepting a supporting role creates an opportunity to let go of judgment, to stop focusing on what we *can't* do and feel good about what we *can* contribute. We choose to support each other and our children despite our differences, and, isn't that what families do?

THIS IS NOT WHAT A FAMILY LOOKS LIKE

"Maybe it's time to let go of what you thought your life would be and begin appreciating it for what it is."

1. Regardless of family structure, we all carry guilt and/or disappointment in regards to our relationships. What stories are you holding on to, stories that you need to let go of?

2. Let's reframe your picture. What *can* you do? What is going well? What are you proud of?

Chapter 5

FEAR SAYS:
"YOU ARE A
TERRIBLE PARENT"

In a late night conversation with Miguel, he suggested my primary emotion (when it comes to parenting) is fear. We had been discussing the immense pressure I put on myself to raise good people. My kids don't have to be brilliant. They don't have to be wealthy, famous, or hold prestigious jobs. I just want them to make responsible choices, be caring and kind, and feel confident about their value and their abilities. No tall order, right? And so, I tend to overanalyze, overthink, and lose sleep about the decisions I make and the conversations I have with my boys.

Surprisingly, when Miguel brought up the idea of fear-based parenting, I had no defense, for I knew he was right. I worry about staying connected to my teenager. I have anxiety about my younger son feeling accepted and valued. I worry about my stepson's happiness. I worry they will be hit by a car, be persuaded by peer pressure, have their brains turned into mush by YouTube and video games. I worry I work too much, that my moments of depression scar them, that my husband and I don't always model a perfect marriage. It's exhausting!

I decided to mention the idea to my therapist, a man who is kind and gentle but incredibly honest. "My husband thinks I parent from a place of fear and I'm afraid he may be right." (Did you catch the irony there? I was *afraid* he was right! Add another layer onto this quadruple-decker fear sandwich.) Leaning back into his cream-colored armchair, my therapist paused for a pensive moment and replied carefully, "Have you ever considered the language you use to talk about yourself?"

Um, I don't think you're listening. We are talking about my parenting, not my self-esteem. How much am I paying this guy?

"When we discuss your husband, your extended family or your children, you are always very empathetic, forgiving their mistakes, giving them the benefit of the doubt. You speak of them with love and kindness. Would you like me to read back some of the phrases you have said about *yourself*?"

This should be interesting, most likely uncomfortable, and certainly humiliating ...

"You have said, and I quote … "I am failing them." "They deserve better than me." "What if they don't know how much I love them?" "It's my fault." "I need to do better." … Shall I continue, or do you get the point?"

Ouch! Hearing my own words read back to me was shocking, and I cried. I would never say such judgmental and hurtful things to another person! Why then, did I say them to myself? My self-talk was laden with criticism and lacked even a smidgen of self-compassion. It seemed I gave grace to everyone, except myself, when it came to making mistakes.

After a moment, a pause to gain my composure, he continued. "What I have learned about you, Kel, is you care an enormous amount about parenting. Probably more than most others. You read, learn, study, and carefully consider each and every decision you make. You consider the well-being of your children, your spouse, your ex-husband and his new family. It is admirable how much you wish to be a good mother. The irony is, you are so consumed by the responsibility of raising your children that it may, in fact, make you a worse parent. Your fear gets in the way, blocking the possibility of living in the moment, experiencing joy and being fully-engaged with your family. Your fear weighs you down, creating exhaustion, anxiety and depression. The hard truth is, despite your best intentions, you are not the mother you want to be, and probably not the mother your children desire."

Double ouch! My ego was taking a beating! And, he wasn't done yet. Breathe, Kel …

"Ironically, the parents who don't necessarily care as much as you, who don't doubt themselves or worry as much, are more relaxed. They are simply happier, and happy parents generally create environments for happy kids. Maybe those parents let their kids watch too much TV or let them eat tons of junk food, or don't help with their homework. But, the parents laugh, smile and play, and their children feel loved and connected. Think about this. When your kids are with you, do they feel your joy or do they feel your stress?"

I hate this guy. I hate him because I know he's right.

I walked out of that session feeling like I had just gone 12 rounds with Mike Tyson. I probably looked like it too, with my puffy face and red, watery eyes. As painful as it was to hear, I was grateful for the perspective. The hard truth usually hurts. I could choose to bury my head in the sand, denying and carrying on as I had been, or I could face the facts head on, lean into discomfort, and work toward change.

I reflected on these thoughts for a few days before wondering if I was the only one who felt afraid all of the time. Surely, I can't be the only parent who struggles with fear. One by one, I consulted my girlfriends, all of them women whom I consider to be amazing mothers. I asked them to consider their primary emotion when it came to parenting. Perhaps, by now, considering the tone of this book, their responses won't be surprising to you. However, at the time, I found their answers simultaneously shocking and comforting. I wasn't alone in my mentality. "Fear" was definitely mentioned. "Guilt" was a close second.

When I step back and look at the big picture, I can see that fear may be the primary emotion for our entire society. It's not just a special badge for parents, earned when you take your baby home from the hospital. None of us can escape the underlying message of fear which permeates our media, our conversations, and our thought patterns. Being privy to American news and culture with such easy access, we are well aware of the culture of mistrust south of the border. It is prevalent in our newscasts, in our music, our movies, our podcasts, and our social media feed. Even in Canada, where tolerance is a quality we strive to practice, many of us don't know our neighbor's names. We walk right past the homeless man on the street, eyes downcast so as not to make contact. We escort our children to school so they won't be hit by a car, lose their way, or be accosted by a stranger. We hesitate to ask questions about the differences of others, for fear of being perceived as ignorant or rude. We are in constant competition for the best house, the nicest car, the most prestigious job. It seems fear has become the undercurrent of our culture, vibrating at such a low frequency that hardly anyone notices. It is no wonder fear runs rampant in the mindset of parents.

We worry our kids won't be accepted into the college of their choice, or make the most exclusive sports team. We fall victim to the pressure of providing them with the best experiences and adventures so they will look back on their childhood and remark how wonderful it was. We run ourselves ragged, driving them to lessons, tutoring and sport practices that will make them well-rounded humans. We work hard to give them material belongings so they will feel as lucky as their peers. We throw lavish birthday parties because our child was invited to so-and-so's event and it's only fair we invite them to ours. We wouldn't want to cause any hurt feelings. We worry about them socially, pray they are included and are treated with kindness. Even worse, we fear it is our kid who will become the bully. We feel guilty when we lose our tempers. We chastise ourselves for working too much and for sending our children to daycare. We struggle to enjoy a night out with our friends or spouse because we should be at home with our kids. We feel guilty when our kids eat scrambled eggs for dinner because we are too tired to make a proper meal.

ENOUGH ALREADY!

Here's the thing. Life is too short to be circling the drain of guilt and fear. The reality is our children are only with us for a limited time. Soon, very soon, they will be off in the world, living their own lives, valuing their peers more than their parents. They will consider our opinions less and less, will share smaller pieces of themselves with us, and experience more when we are not around. They will become busy with after-school activities, with studies, with jobs, with new friends and first loves. It's scary, but it's natural. All teenagers separate from their parents in an effort to figure out who they are. If they are brave enough to venture out into the world, it means we have done our job right. That's not to say the sting of missing them doesn't hurt. I am beginning to feel this pressure. My oldest son is almost 14 years old, and I am keenly aware that in three or four years, he will be gone. That's all I have. Three or four years. And I am wasting that time being worried and tired.

Truthfully, as parents, we can never step completely away from fear. When a piece of you is walking in this world, finding his or her own way, this level of trust requires an enormous amount of faith that everything will be alright. I can't ask you to let go of your fears. It would simply be an impossible and unreasonable request—like asking you to hold a cloud in your hands. But that doesn't mean we shouldn't try. The preservation of my mental sanity requires me to loosen my grip on the fear that keeps me in the darkness. I need to take a deep breath, have faith, and walk toward the light. Holding on to my worries will not only cause me to lose my mind, but also create a disconnect with my children, the people I love the most. I get lost inside my head easily, weighed down by my concerns, planning and preparing for the worst-case scenario. I spend hours thinking of ways to protect, to avoid disaster, and to emotionally prepare myself and my children, so we may survive the inevitable pain. In these moments, I am gone, lost in contemplation, unavailable to my children who are standing right in front of me. I need to turn down the volume of my worries so I may find more joy.

When my children are grown, I don't want them to think about their mother and remark how nervous I was, how serious or grouchy, how fearful. I want them to think about me and remember how loved they felt, how trusted and supported they were. This is my motivation to change. I need to simultaneously hold space for my fear while also rising above it.

The consequences of *not* rising above could be potentially devastating. Children are perceptive and can sense fear like a woman with PMS sniffing out a chocolate bar. If I'm afraid, will my children feel safe and secure sharing their own struggles with me? Will my teenage son feel confident, calling his mother in the middle of the night when he needs a safe ride home, or will he fear my irrational reaction? Will my younger boy share his friendship struggles at school, or will he hold them close, not wanting his mommy to be upset? Uncontrolled fear closes the lines of communication and undercuts the trust we work so hard to build. I must do better. The alternative is simply not an option.

Your logical brain probably agrees with every word I wrote in this chapter. *I* agree with the logic of it. However, we both know, emotionally, it's a tall order. The question becomes how do we become the parents we wish to be, despite our fears?

What the Warrior Says:

LESSON 1:
YOU ARE NOT, IN FACT, A TERRIBLE PARENT!

"A warrior can train for battle, spending hours each day perfecting her sword skills. A warrior listens to her mentor and meditates so her mind is strong. A warrior pours over battle plans and envisions herself a fearless soldier. And, do you know what happens, as the battle cry sounds and chaos erupts? The Warrior hears the screams, sees the bloodshed and stands for a moment in fear. Then, she remembers to trust in herself, her intuition, and her preparedness, and goes forth to kick ass. It's not unlike parenting."

Did you feed your child today? Did you make sure they got to school? Did you kiss them or hug them? Did you ask how their day was? Yes? Congratulations, you are a good parent!

Did you guide your children through their mistakes? Did you tell them how much you love them and enjoy their company? Did you attend their play, their recital or their game? Did you tuck them in at night? Congratulations, you are an exceptional parent!

Think about how you were raised. How many of you would claim to be raised by good parents? Probably most of us can say we had a good-enough childhood, or at the very least, understand that our parents did their very best. Do you honestly think our parents worried as much as we do about their children's emotional well-being? Mine didn't! They told me to go outside, get out of their hair, and come back when it was time for dinner. And guess, what?! I still knew, undoubtedly, that they loved me. My parents did not plan play dates for us. They didn't take it personally when we were bored. They were not home every day after school. They sure didn't read parenting magazines or listen to expert advice. And I turned out just fine. Mostly.

The fact you even stop to consider your own parenting practices proves you are not a bad parent. Taking a moment to think about how your attitudes, trauma, and perspectives affect your children, shows how much you care. The fact you are willing to set aside ego and evaluate your actions shows your level of dedication. Your decision to do the hard work and strive toward change is amazing. Don't you forget it!

We put so much pressure on ourselves to be perfect and all it does is create toxic pressure which becomes heavier and heavier. As our children grow older and become adolescents, parenting becomes increasingly complicated. Decisions are rarely black and white, for teenagers seem to operate exclusively in shades of grey. This obscurity can be very confusing. When my children were little, I was a confident parent, yet as they mature, I feel as if I'm crossing my fingers, hoping I only screw up a little.

"Mommy, can I have more milk?"

"Mommy, can I play outside?"

"Mommy, can I stay up a little later tonight?"

"Mommy, can I go to the park by myself?"

"Mom, can I go to that concert?"

"Mom, I'm failing Math. What should I do?"

"Mom, I'm not happy. Can I change schools?"

"Mom, my friend ran away from home. Why would he do that?"

"Mom, there are drugs at this party. Can you come pick me up?"

It happens so fast it's almost impossible to sense the moment when it shifts—the moment when you cease being a caregiver and start becoming a guide. Inevitably, there comes a time when our role as parents change, when we need to let go of control and let our children experience life without their hands being held. We need to let our children make mistakes and learn from the consequences. We need to trust we have raised good kids, ones that know right from wrong. We need to let them go, let them explore, let them get hurt. This realization can be terrifying.

In response to my newfound discomfort in terms of parenting, my therapist challenged me to "only give a little shit" about things—a concept I have grown to love. He observed that I tend to give an enormous shit about everything. Every decision I made felt like a big deal and the weight of it was crushing. I had convinced myself I was capable of carrying that weight, that it was part and parcel of being a responsible parent. I told myself it was a noble burden. This "noble burden" had become so cumbersome, I could no longer carry it with grace. I needed a new strategy, one that would free me and allow some space for joy. What if every time I felt anxious about parenting, I took a moment to remember I have invested 13 years into raising wonderful children? I have taught them to have opinions, to seek advice from others, to be kind, to be curious, to be confident. Now, I need to step back a little and trust they can handle themselves. I need to give them some power and control, allow them room to make mistakes and understand that those mistakes are not a reflection on my parenting. Nor are they a measure of how much I love them. Yes, I will always worry and care about my children, but that worry does not need to be enormous every single day—hence, only giving a little shit.

If that sentiment doesn't register with you or make you laugh, as it did for me, try this on for size. I also believe in the power of self-forgiveness and self-compassion. Navigating parenting is tricky for me these days. How much freedom do I allow? How much do I step back and allow my children to make mistakes? How often will I lose my temper or impose my anxiety onto my children? I have learned to be honest with myself and with my kids. The truth is, I have never raised a teenager before. I am not always sure of what I am doing. My younger son, though not a teenager quite yet, is very different from his brother. What worked for my older child does not always work for my youngest. I have never been a step-mother before. I may not always navigate the complexity of that relationship with grace. The bottom line is I am going to make mistakes and I share this truth with my children. We are all learning together. Most days, they will forgive my transgressions. Children, after all, love their parents and generally have a short memory when it comes to our faults. (Thank the lord!) Now, I need to work on forgiving *myself* for the moments and days when I am not perfect.

Being imperfect does not make me a terrible parent. It makes me a normal one.

LESSON 2:
YOUR CHILDREN WANT TO SEE YOU HAPPY.

"Did you forget that you need to show your children how to live? They watch you, forming lifelong ideas about what it means to be a parent, a person and a spouse. They observe, and they create ideas about selfishness, selflessness, happiness and unhappiness. Show them that taking care of themselves is a form of love, of leadership and of necessity. Teach them that they are responsible for creating their own misery and, in turn, manifesting their own joy. Be the person you wish for them to become."

My children don't care that I read parenting magazines. They don't care that I carefully consider the healthiest foods to feed them. They wouldn't like the fact that I cry myself to sleep with worry or that I pace the house in the middle of the night, wondering how to be a good mother.

They don't really care that we drive a crappy car or that their friends go on more vacations than we do. They don't mind being home alone for an hour or two after school while I am at work. They enjoy going to their grandparent's house so I can have a carefree weekend away.

What they *do* care about are the moments when their mother is stuck in her head and emotionally unavailable. They notice the days when I don't laugh, smile, or have the energy to play. They feel the stress that radiates when I am overworked and overtired. They suffer the sting of my short temper and my salty moods.

The truth is, my kids are happy when I am happy. When I am relaxed, their world feels safe. When I am joyful, I am available to connect on an emotional and playful level. When my mind is free from worry, I can engage with them, diving deep into conversation and enjoying their curiosity and silliness. At the end of the day, my kids just want a happy mom.

When they become adults and look back on their childhood, I know my boys won't remark at the thoughtfulness of my parenting, recalling the hours of contemplation and careful decision-making. I hope they don't remember their mother as a stressed out, hot mess of a woman who always looked exhausted and upset. I want them to think about how much I loved them and remember the adventures we had together. How do you want your children to remember you?

The legacy I want to leave behind, for my boys, are memories filled with love, laughter and joy. With this in mind, I realize I need to let go of a long list of thoughts that don't serve me:

- Guilt over being a busy, working mother or being overtired and/or overwhelmed.

- Fear of making mistakes.

- Guilt that I am not deserving of self-fulfillment or self-care.

- Worry that my kids deserve a better mom.

- Fear of loss of control and ability to protect my children from harm.

Instead, I would like to commit to the following thoughts:

- I deserve to laugh, to dance, to play with my children. They deserve a mom who is relaxed and engaged.

- I am going to make mistakes and everything will be okay.

- I choose to give a "little shit" about most problems and worries.

- I deserve to be happy and need to engage in self-care routines.

- My children are smart and responsible. They will be okay.

Take a moment to investigate your self-talk. Is it serving you or harming you? Are you self-chastising, like I was? Does your inner voice whisper that you are failing as a parent or as a spouse? What emotions are weighing you down? Once you become aware of the stories you are telling yourself, you can find the power to rewire the thought loop.

You are not a terrible parent, nor am I. We are merely guilt-laden martyrs who are doing the very best we can on any given day. I don't know about you, but I am sick and tired of being a guilt-laden martyr. It's no fun! Being a martyr is a heavy, serious responsibility and it blocks all possible joy. The thing is, nobody asked me to play that role. Nobody forced me or suggested, "Hey Kel, you should feel really badly about your parenting." Nope. It was all me, a role I designated for myself. Or, more accurately, a role Fear signed me up for.

I know I am making all of this sound glib, or easy, as if you can just choose to change your mentality with a snap of your fingers or the click of ruby slippers. It won't be easy but don't let that be an excuse not to try. I will always overthink my parenting and worry about my children. The difference now is that I have become aware of my tendency to let those concerns weigh me down and rob me of true happiness and connection. My goal is not to become a completely different person. That's unattainable. No, my goal is to catch myself when I fall back into old habits and correct my mindset when needed. I will need to consciously remind myself that I am a great parent and that I deserve to feel positive about myself and my efforts. These self-corrections occur often, at first. But the hope is, over time, my mind will naturally gravitate toward joy without needing frequent reminders and I will start to believe my own mantras.

I AM A TERRIBLE PARENT

"She remembers to trust in herself, her intuition and her preparedness and goes forth to kick ass."

1. What are your parenting fears?

2. How do these fears affect you and/or your children on a daily basis?

3. If you could let go of these fears, what would your life feel like?

4. What self-care routines have you built in, so you can show up as an engaged and connected parent?

Chapter 6

FEAR SAYS:

"YOU ARE NOT WORTHY"

Every August, I have the same dream. The specifics may vary slightly, but the tone and overriding message return summer after summer and cause me to bolt upright in bed, drenched in sweat. I am standing at the front of a classroom, while students hurl paper airplanes across the room, and wrestle on the floor, bodies pretzeled and arms flailing. They stand on desks, shouting obscenities. I desperately try to get their attention and fight to gain control, to no avail. I am powerless in the face of these unruly children. Panic rises within me, a bead of sweat drips—in slow motion—down my forehead, just as I hear the footsteps of the principal beating down the hallway. He's coming. And, he's going to discover the secret I have been keeping all these years. I am, in fact, a terrible teacher.

I have had some version of this dream during the week before school every single year, *for 15 freaking years!*

I'm sure a psychotherapist would love to analyze this dream and could tap into a whole host of control issues, ramble on about my self-confidence and speculate about my feelings of having no voice. What I choose to focus on, however, is the inherent lack of self-worth and the non-existent belief in myself.

In reality, I am damn good at what I do and I'm not afraid to say it. I have walked into chaotic classrooms, like the one in my dream, and quickly calmed the nuthouse. I train new teachers and speak at professional development seminars for even the most experienced educators. I am passionate about teaching and have dedicated my whole adult life to mastering my craft. Teaching is not my job. It is a part of who I am at my core.

So why, then, does my deepest subconscious mind like to suggest I am a fraud? Why does my emotional self suggest I am unworthy of the well-respected professional reputation I have worked diligently for years to cultivate? It's because I am afraid. I am afraid if people got to know the real me, I would never be able to live up to the idealized version of myself that I have created. The real me would be a let-down, a colossal disappointment. If you were to strip away the accolades and the professional confidence … If you were to hang up the nice clothes and see me in my flannel pajamas … If you were to separate me from my labels: mother, daughter, teacher, writer, speaker … If you were to wipe off my makeup and I was forced to stand with nothing else to hide behind ... I fear you might find me boring. And an insecure mess of a human being.

Am I the only one who feels this way? Am I not enough without the bright, shiny distractions I have created? The need for illusions reminds me of the scene at the end of The Wizard of Oz, when Dorothy stands, in awe, in front of the great and powerful Oz, smoke billowing, voice booming, only to discover a moment later, a small, insignificant man hiding behind all the smoke and mirrors. Sadly, I cannot remember the end of the movie. Is she left utterly unimpressed by his lack of gravitas? Or does she remind both him and herself that he is a normal person, deserving of respect just as he is and doesn't need to distract others with a silly diversion?

In truth, like the Great and Powerful Oz, I have spent much of my adult life hoping not to be found out.

I wouldn't classify myself as an introvert entirely, nor an extrovert either. I hover somewhere in the middle, excelling in my comfort zones and strapping on my Game Face when pushed outside my boundaries. Large gatherings make me uncomfortable—meetings, corporate events, parties even. I'm not good at small talk because I don't consider myself to be particularly witty or entertaining. I'm not one to tell a story (ironic). I've most definitely never told a joke. I can't sell myself in two minutes or less. Where I excel is in meaningful conversation. I am an excellent listener. I truly want to know all about someone—about their job, their family, their dreams. Put me in a coffee shop with a warm mug in my hand (or on a couch with a blanket and a glass of wine) when we have hours to chat and get to know each other, and I am in my element!

By now, you've read about many aspects of my life, aspects which are tainted by this theme, the worry that I am not enough. Fear affects my social comfort level, my marriage, my parenting, and my relationship with my parents. I am, indeed, an expert at self-deprecation—a thought loop I have been working my way out of for years. In the past, this negative self-image has also caused me to limit my dreams and to think small. I am a dreamer by nature, incredibly driven and ambitious. However, I was always nervous to share my goals with others, for fear of judgment. Because, who am I to deserve it all? Maybe I should just stick to what I know I'm good at, and be grateful for the blessings I already have.

I know this all sounds whiny. It's not that I'm ungrateful. In fact, it's the very opposite. I know I have been blessed in so many ways, so it seems audacious to ask for more. Yet, the voice is there. It's a voice I've always heard. It whispers faintly, at the back of my consciousness, only audible in moments of stillness and silence. "*You are meant for more.*" I heard it in the years and months leading up to my divorce. "*You are meant for more.*" I heard it in the final years and months of my teaching career. "*You are meant for more.*" I heard it after I published my first book, a triumph I never in my wildest dreams thought I would experience. "*You are meant for more.*" The voice scares me, terrifies me, yet drives me forward at the same time. When I hear the voice, I know it's true, but self-doubt kicks in almost immediately. "Who are you to deserve more?"

There are so many reasons not to follow my dreams and become a full-time writer and motivational speaker. Coming across as a whiny, ungrateful bitch isn't even in the top five! Here are a few little gems which plague my motivation:

Excuse #1: Fear of failure looms largely and ominously. Once you share an ambition, there is a certain level of accountability to it. If I hold my dreams close to my chest, carrying them in secret, no one will know if I don't achieve them or don't chase them at all. When everything comes secretly crashing down, only I will know how much I suck.

Excuse #2: I consider myself to be a late bloomer, starting a new career at 40 years old. I try to remind myself I have spent my younger years gathering the experience which grants me the knowledge I have today. But, I fear society may not be accepting of a woman with wrinkles as well as wisdom. Wouldn't you rather look at the fresh-faced smile and tight booty of a 30 year old motivational speaker?

Excuse #3: I have responsibilities! Humiliation is not the only byproduct of a career failure. There's also the looming threat of the inability to pay my mortgage or send my kids to college. No biggie.

I recently had a series of conversations with different friends whose skyrocketing careers and personal fierceness inspire me. In each conversation, a question was asked which struck me, causing me to re-evaluate the limits fear has caused me to place upon myself. I'll share them with you now, and we will re-visit them in the journaling section at the end of this chapter.

I am lucky enough to have found a mentor, who is a brilliant author, speaker, branding expert, and CEO of her own company. She's a badass! In guiding me to create a clear and tangible vision for my future career and life goals, she said, "If I could wave a magic wand and give you the career and life you truly desire, what would that look like?" The question was overwhelming, having a blank slate to envision a life that would be professionally and personally fulfilling. Despite initially being dumbfounded by her inquiry, deep down I knew the answer because it had been stirring inside me for months, yet speaking it aloud felt ridiculous and I was embarrassed to admit my truest desires. I had written them, daily, over and over in my journal in an attempt to manifest something in The Universe, yet saying them out loud *to another person* felt very vulnerable. I pushed through my fear and shared them. To her credit, she did not laugh or scoff. She asked what I was doing to move that dream forward and asked what she could do to help. Her calm and supportive response immediately made me feel that although my dreams are lofty, they are not ridiculous. In fact, they may be entirely attainable, as long as I remain patient, persistent and hard working.

Weeks later, I was chatting with another friend who, like me, is a big dreamer. I was sharing the wisdom I had received from the conversation with my mentor, telling him of my ambitions to create a life where I am a bestselling author and travelling the country and speaking to people about my stories.

"Why wouldn't you travel the world, Kel?" he asked.

"Huh?"

"You said you want to travel the country and I presume, in your head, you are speaking to small groups of a hundred or two hundred people. Why wouldn't you travel the world and stand on stage in front of thousands?"

I laughed at that suggestion. "I'm surprised *anyone* wants to read my books and hear my speeches! I know I have a lot to share, but I am always afraid no one will listen. If people show up, that's an automatic win and if they pay me, that's the cherry on the ice cream sundae!"

"Why are you putting a ceiling on your dreams?" he asked. "If you believe thousands or millions of people should read your work, then that will happen. If you believe your wisdom is worth a lot, people will pay to hear you speak. If you don't hold these beliefs for yourself, how can you ever expect to be successful?"

These two conversations—happening in short succession of each other—seemed like a message from The Universe. (Yes, I am *that* girl, the one who looks for cosmic signs.) I shouldn't be afraid to dream big, for I can only achieve the goals I truly commit myself to. If I don't take ownership of what I really want, if I make a half-assed attempt to chase my dreams, they most certainly won't come true. And, why *not* ask for it all? If I feel a pull toward a life larger than the one I am currently living, why deny that longing? Why put a ceiling on future possibilities and unknown potential?

Who cares if people judge? My dreams and ambitions are mine. They don't belong to anyone but me, and don't need to be understood by anyone but me. Not everyone, after all, is a big dreamer, or is brave enough to go after what they truly desire. For some, playing it safe is what brings them comfort. That's just not for me. I need to stop asking permission! Making myself small to make others comfortable will only breed regret. I would rather fail miserably attempting to achieve my dreams, rather than ignore my inner yearnings just so I don't appear to others to be full of myself. I want to be able to look back and say, "Well, at least I went for it."

If I am lucky enough to create my ideal reality one day, my success will be the result of having worked my ass off to achieve it. My achievements will have been built on blood, sweat and tears. I will be worthy of that reward.

However, I need to ask myself, "If I chase my dreams and fail, and if everything remained the same as it is today, would it be enough? Would *I* be enough?" The answer is *yes*. I may not be a world-renowned author and speaker, but I will be courageous. I will be proud of myself for trying. No matter what happens, I will always be a loving wife, daughter, friend, and mother. I will always be a good person. This will never change.

I am enough.

What the Warrior Says:

LESSON 1:
WE ALL HAVE A THOUGHT LOOP.

*"Sometimes you need to tell yourself to shut the hell up. The inner
messaging that plays on repeat, is not who you are. It's separate
from you and it can be silenced, manipulated or rearranged.
Language is powerful and if your thoughts aren't serving you,
then change them. When fear creeps in and whispers that you
aren't enough, tell fear to shove it. You are a Warrior. Let this be
your mantra."*

My internal voice is a negative one. It tells me I'm a fraud. I
am boring. I am a terrible mother. I'm not a good wife. My
inner thought loop suggests I am not worthy of the lovely life I
have created, nor of achieving my ambitious hopes and dreams.
This inner voice is my prime motivator for working hard on
my career and my relationships. I want to prove I am worth
everything I have been blessed with.

While this internal dialogue inspires me to work hard and be
a good person, it does so in a messed up way—in a way that
affects my self-esteem, my mental health and it creates a fear
of being discovered. Yep, I suffer from imposter syndrome!
Constantly working to prove one's worth and hiding deficiencies
is exhausting.

It's worth investigating where our thought loops come from. A
childhood trauma? Birth order? Perceived social or professional
slights? Messages we misconstrued along the way? Usually, our

internal dialogue can be traced back to some deep-seeded core belief we weren't even aware we had. For me, somewhere in my childhood, I began to associate success with love. Couple my first-born status, with an overachieving and ambitious personality and you have a perfect recipe for collecting accolades. My parents would proudly share my victories with friends and family. My dad would take me for dinner when I earned a perfect report card—a rare and special treat with my parents' modest income. I basked in the glory of my parents' attention and praise. Even as an adult, when my parents speak about my professional achievements or remark to others how charming my children are, I glow unabashedly. They noticed my hard work. They noticed *me*. Though I know they would have loved me no matter what my report card said, at some point, my developing brain connected the synapses linking love and success. This mindset puts an incredible amount of pressure on a person because if success equals love, failure must equate to being unlovable. It's no wonder my core fears are that I am not enough and that I am unworthy of true acceptance. Once I was able to articulate those beliefs and unpack them further, I began to realize how ludicrous and untrue they were.

My parents offered many examples of love, ones that weren't based on my success. My mom and dad were affectionate, supportive and playful. They never withdrew love or affection upon failure. Someone recently asked me why the childhood memories of accomplishment stand out in my mind instead of quiet, calm moments. The truth is, I hold countless memories of my childhood with affection. I can recall climbing trees in my yard, camping in the forest, baking with my dad, putting on my mother's makeup and doing crafts with her. I don't know why my brain holds those memories with sweet tenderness and memories of achievement with ferocity and extra weight. My only tentative answer is that a child's perception is what it is. Perhaps it can't be explained—only examined, unpacked and corrected later in life.

My mother is always the first person to read my work. I often send her my first draft, a book in its infancy, and ask for her initial reactions to it. She graciously reads everything twice— once to allow herself room for emotional reactions to the words, and again with a keen literary eye. After she read this chapter, she called me.

"The dinners with your dad were not a reward for good grades. Didn't you know that? They were a celebration of the completion of another school year, a kick-off to summer vacation. If you had gotten a poor report card, we still would have bought you dinner."

It's funny how perception, especially from a young child, can skew the truth and morph people's intentions into something else. These misperceptions become the lifelong stories we tell ourselves and the reality is, they aren't even true. Yet we carry these misperceptions around, allowing them to shape our self-esteem, our value, and our worth. My parents would have been proud of me no matter what I decided to become in life, as long as I was happy.

So, the question becomes, once we are aware of the stories our internal voice whispers and the seeds of fear it plants, how do we overcome and rise above? I believe language has the power to reset our brains. We need to pay attention to the negative language we use when referencing ourselves. When we notice our negative self-talk, we need to stop it and replace it with words that serve us well and build us up instead of tear us down. I practice this in a number of ways.

- I begin my day by writing in a gratitude journal. Instead of being uncomfortable with my blessings and feeling undeserving of them, I choose to be grateful and thank The Universe for smiling upon me in small and countless ways.

- I use positive affirmations in times when I am feeling uncertain. "I deserve this. I have worked hard for this. I am kind and thoughtful. I am a caring friend, a compassionate mother, an empathetic wife, a dedicated professional."

- I meditate and chant mantras. When we speak things aloud in a confident way, we put the vibration into The Universe and manifest our destiny. (This sentiment may be a bit out there for some of you, but don't check out! See it through!) Firstly, when we speak our thoughts aloud, there is a certain level of accountability. We are owning them! Writing them down serves the same purpose and sets an intention of commitment. These are not just dreams, they are attainable goals. Secondly, using language of success, belief, and confidence wires those thoughts in our brains so they become our thought loop. I might say, "I will find a way to make my dreams a reality." (Not "I *hope* to find a way." But "I *will* find a way.") "I will become a successful writer." "I am going to show up as a good mother and wife today." "I am a calm and joyful person." These things, repeated over and over, become my reality.

LESSON 2:
IF YOU LOVE YOURSELF, OTHERS WILL FOLLOW, BECAUSE YOU ARE FREAKING AMAZING.

"Need I say more?"

I AM NOT WORTHY

"You are a Warrior. Need I say more?"

1. If I could wave a magic wand and give you the life and career you long for, what would that look like?

2. What's holding you back from claiming that reality?

3. What mantras can you ingrain in your brain to carry you toward success?

Chapter 7

FEAR SAYS:
"YOU ARE DEPRESSION"

Okay, I'm about to get really vulnerable with you, not my regular approach. I promise to strip away The Game Face and stand naked before you, raw and exposed. It's terrifying, but I'm choosing to lean into the discomfort because I know I am not alone in this struggle and I truly believe there is value in open and honest conversation. Someone, somewhere, needs to hear this. I am willing to push past my fear and share my most secretive truth. Lord help me.

I have struggled with bouts of depression, off and on, for most of my adult life. While I have carefully crafted a bright and shiny exterior shell that protects both my image and my ego, on the inside, I am a swirling storm with dark, heavy cloud cover. When I began to share stories of my depression, people who have known me for years were shocked and surprised. When it comes to talking about my truth, I had become an expert at deflection, redirection, and flat out lying. "Oh my God, I am so great! Life is just awesome! Enough about me. Let's talk about you!"

I am not always a black, angry cloud. Some days, I am shades of gray, wispy clouds that make for a warm, but overcast day. Other times, I am white and fluffy, resting on a brilliant blue backdrop. My depression can lie dormant for years, leaving me to believe I've conquered it, but just when I relax a little, it rears its ugly head once again. The funny thing is I don't always see it coming because, like a sneaky little shape-shifter, it manifests in different forms. Sometimes, it's a feeling of being completely overwhelmed by life. Sometimes, I cry for days. Sometimes, I am too exhausted to get out of bed. Sometimes, I have anxiety. Sometimes, I have stomach aches or insomnia. Sometimes, I think it's just stress. Sometimes, I feel empty, as if all feelings have vacated my body. But I know it's bad when the voice in my head morphs into someone I don't like.

I know what I am about to tell you may make me sound crazy. You might think, "Why am I taking life advice from this unstable chick?" Call me unstable, if you like. I sure feel that way sometimes! However, in my more lucid moments (pardon my sarcasm), I try to reflect and think about what The Universe is trying to teach me. And, like I've said, somebody needs to be brave enough to put all of their shit out there, so everyone else can feel a little more normal for half a second.

Sorry. I'm being defensive. It's my "go to" when the only other option is vulnerability.

Here's the thing. There are moments, days, weeks or even months, when my inner dialogue is nasty. It doesn't even sound like me or feel like me. In fact, I consider it a separate entity. Like Satan has set up camp in my brain, with his cozy fire pit, tin cup of whisky and a worn-out banjo. His entertainment (other than the drinking and twangy banjo music)? Messing with my mind. Day after day, he points out negativities, hints at my inadequacy, and spews hateful words about myself and others.

I acknowledge I am using humour to deflect. Again, sorry.

There are moments when I don't feel in control of my brain and it's scary. Terrifying, actually. I don't trust what I am going to say. I don't know how I will react. When I hear hateful words swirling inside my mind, I have to stop and tell myself not to fall prey to Satan's games. It's a constant battle to block out his propaganda and focus on gratitude, positivity, and strength. At times, I feel like a shell of a person, outwardly performing normally. Remember to smile. That was funny, you should laugh. Say hello. Be polite. But underneath the trendy shirt, social niceties and pretty pink lipstick, a war is raging. Sometimes, I lose the battle.

The lucky winner and unsuspecting recipient of my toxicity is, unfortunately, one of my favorite people, my husband. My defenses are fatigued after spending all day navigating a high-energy, high-paced classroom environment. However, I can usually hold myself together in the presence of my own children.

I'm not perfect and I do lose my patience with them, or even disengage from time to time when I become overwhelmed. Most days, I fight hard to be present for them and to protect them from the negativity bubbling, like molten lava, inside my mind. My worst fear, after all, would be to lose control of my emotional state and scar them. If I do anything right in this life, it will be to negate the impact my depression has on my kids. I expend copious amounts of my emotional reserves trying to be a great mom. By the end of a long, hectic day, I am depleted. It's in those moments, when I am alone with the love of my life, when Satan becomes unleashed and Miguel has to face his ferocity. I take things too personally and react with anger or defensiveness. I lose my patience when my darling husband asks for clarification or help. I cry hysterically from exhaustion or use strong language because I feel backed into a corner. It's not charming.

In my work, I often remind parents that their children behave badly in their presence because parents represent a safety zone. Their children have spent all day working hard to be social, to regulate their emotions, and to comply with societal expectations of behavior. When they finally see their parents, they are tired! Parents, who have eagerly looked forward to seeing their children at the end of a long and busy day, are not greeted by sweet, smiling cherubs. No, inside their homes are tantruming, nose-dripping, red cheeked demons who are screaming for attention, food, and television. You see, the kids know their parents will love them unconditionally. Just like most adults I know, children also need a stress release, and they know their parents will show up the next day, despite their unruly behavior. It seems that Miguel is my safe person. Lucky him. He deserves a medal. Or an enormous trophy. Or a shirt that says, "I survived Satan and all I got was this lousy t-shirt."

When I lash out at Miguel, I know I have let Satan get the best of me. My husband knows it too, and he tries not to take it personally, yet it still hurts him. He'll look at me, with tears in his eyes and say, "I know that wasn't you, Kel." Pull the dagger out of my tiny heart and let the shame bleed down my chest. Kindness when I don't deserve it is the absolute worst. There are so many moments when I feel shame and guilt, when I know my husband deserves a better wife than me. I wish I could be that person for him, yet, here I am, I screwed up again. Because Miguel is familiar with my struggles, he forgives me again and again. He knows I love him and he knows how hard I am fighting during these times. The depth of his empathy and compassion is astounding. Not a day goes by without a moment of gratitude for this man, strong and understanding, who stays with me during my darkest moments. He doesn't judge my crazy, but I know his heart aches for me.

The Game Face has served me well over the years, helped hide my pain and shield others from its wrath. In truth, when I am around others, I am usually capable of finding moments of joy. It's probably why I restlessly seek quality time with my friends and family. I can enjoy a sunny afternoon on the beach with my children. I can appreciate an interesting workshop with colleagues. I relish belly laughs with girlfriends. It's as if Satan is momentarily distracted (by stoking his fire or topping up his whisky) and I am able to catch a glimpse of who I am meant to be. As joyful as those moments are, these little glimpses of my true self break my heart, for that person seems just out of reach to my outstretched fingers. She's there. I can see her. I can feel her presence. But I can't *be* her for more than an hour or two.

It's in moments of quiet stillness, times without distraction, when I am left to ponder my own thoughts. I wonder if I'm normal. I wonder if other people need to work this hard to maintain composure. I wonder if others are putting on a front, as I am, or if they are truly as happy as they appear. I wonder if the boiling resentment inside me is a treatable symptom of depression, or if it's truly who I am at my core. Maybe, I'm not depressed. Maybe I am an unkind, miserable human being. Now, there's a truly disturbing thought. In the moments when I lose trust in myself and in the kind of person I am, I try to remember that most unsavory folks don't carry this much remorse, nor do they have a desire to be better, to do better.

The reason I write this chapter is twofold. Firstly, I want you to know that if you are a person who battles depression, I stand with you. I commend your efforts to get out of bed in the morning. I cheer you on as you make breakfast for your children and take them to school. I high-five you as you perform your professional duties to the best of your ability. I am proud of you, as you kiss your spouse and show affection to those you love. My heart also breaks for you because I know the pain you hide. I want you to know, you are not alone.

Let me say it again. You are not alone.

Very few of us are brave enough to admit we struggle. I'm damn sure one of your colleagues has anxiety. Someone in your family struggles with self-worth. One of your friends falls into depression from time to time. We are out there, walking alongside you. You just don't see us because we are masters of disguise. When all else fails, think of me. I am in the trenches with you and together we will beat this.

I hope you build a support system and trust a handful of people with your pain. Talk to a girlfriend, a sibling, a parent, a therapist. Talk to your cat, if it helps! I have learned the hard way. When we keep our pain a secret, we essentially build a pressure cooker which will explode unpredictably at any time. Feelings are funny that way. They tend to seep through the cracks or detonate like a bomb. If you don't deal with your emotions, they will find a way out.

I hope you develop some coping methods. Talk a brisk walk. Head to the gym. Meditate. Medicate, if you need to. Self-care is absolutely essential! Women, especially, tend to feel guilty about looking after themselves. I say, screw that! We can't pour from an empty cup. If you are not okay, your kids are not okay. If you are crumbling, so is your marriage. Taking time for yourself and your mental health is not a luxury. It is a goddamn necessity! Stop beating yourself up and go for that massage!

Secondly, if you are a person who is in love with someone battling depression, bless your beautiful soul. I can only imagine how helpless you must feel and how hard it must be to remain strong and forgiving. Please, please remember this—it's not personal. It probably feels personal when your loved one shuts you out, acts irrationally, or lashes out. It must be lonely, going to events alone because your spouse can't get out of bed. Miguel has often said he misses me because the wife he knows and loves is absent. It breaks my heart and, if I could change it, I would. No one wants to be depressed. No one chooses depression.

I am making the executive decision to speak on behalf of all who suffer from depression and tell you this. We are terrified you will leave us and we wouldn't blame you if you did. In fact, we believe we would deserve it. It kills us to know we are hurting you. Though we may not be fully in control of our behavior, we do feel the ramifications of it, and this creates a negative shame spiral. We love you more than we love ourselves. I say this, not to incite guilt on your part, but hopefully to instill some understanding and empathy. Our depressive behavior is truly, truly not about you, even if it seems to be.

It must be incredibly difficult to have to be the "strong one", picking up the slack, constantly forgiving and forgetting. I can't even imagine the levels of frustration and hurt you must feel. You are a saint, my friend. Might I suggest you take a moment to re-read the paragraph on self-care. You need to put on your own oxygen mask before saving others. Don't feel badly about taking a moment for yourself. You need it as much as, or more than the next guy. But please take a moment to reassure your loved one you adore them and will be back once you have replenished your own spirit.

I hope, above all, you remember the following sentiment, this, too, shall pass. Encourage your loved one to seek help. Take care of yourself and have faith this difficult season will not last forever. With proper care, depression is curable. I promise. And, I thank you, from the bottom of my heart, for your compassion, your patience, and your unconditional love.

What the Warrior Says:

LESSON 1:
IT'S OKAY NOT TO BE OKAY.

"Sometimes life is ugly. Sometimes we are ugly, and it's okay.
Sometimes life is brutal. Sometimes we are brutal, and it's okay.
Sometimes life just sucks. Sometimes we just suck, and it's okay.
What's not okay is denying ourselves the space to feel the pain."

As I stated, before I began writing, publishing all of my issues for the world to read, most people had no idea I struggled with my mental health. Whenever people asked how I was doing, my response was always positive and "socially acceptable", even if I was hurting on the inside. As a result, I often found myself emotionally isolated. After my divorce, for example, I carried an enormous amount of guilt over the hurt I had caused my husband, so I encouraged our friends and family to reach out and support him. Since the decision to leave had been mine, I felt I should suffer quietly and was not deserving of people's love and attention at that difficult moment. When our friends and family asked how I was coping, I would reply I was okay and then bury myself in my hibernation hole, be antisocial and shut out the world. Truth be told, I was not okay. I was scared, lonely, and guilt-ridden. Though I am sure my friends didn't believe my declarations of being strong and confident in my choices, they eventually stopped checking in. They stopped asking how I was or if I needed anything. And then, I was truly alone in my suffering. The only person I could blame for that was myself.

After writing my last book—which broadcast my struggles like a flag above a castle—I was taken aback by people's positive reactions to my honesty and vulnerability. No one judged me. They applauded me! For the first time in my adult life, I felt empowered by the realization that people would accept me for who I truly am, warts and all.

Admitting I have moments when I am not okay is not only a healthy and important aspect of my emotional intelligence, but also opens the door for meaningful connection with others. Admitting I am not okay and reserving judgment in that confession creates space for self-compassion and self-forgiveness. It alleviates the pressure to be perfect and evaporates the necessity to be fake. All of these gains allow me to be authentic in my relationships—relationships that are growing deeper and richer due to my imperfections. Forcing myself to walk through life with a false smile only served to perpetuate my depression, to keep me feeling alone, unsafe and misunderstood. As soon as I let that fake smile fall from my face, openly cried tears and admitted my fears, the weight of having to "have it all together" disappeared from my shoulders. I felt lighter. Freer.

LESSON 2:
THIS IS NOT MY FAULT.

"The Universe handed you depression because it knows you can handle it. It knows you are strong enough to fight and resilient enough to overcome. Don't mistake depression as a weakness. It is not your choice. It is not your fault, but it is the battleground where you will find out what you are really made of."

There is a shame that accompanies depression. A desperate need to hide and suffer secretly. That may, in fact, be the most painful part of this experience. The pressure to appear as if I have it all together—even when the dark waters are swirling within me—is exhausting. Most days, I feel like a fraud, as if no one knows the real me. I will never let them see the turmoil storming inside, the negativity and confusion that bubbles like poison. I will never let them know.

I tell myself vulnerability should be endearing, a Disney-like version of sorrow that would inspire empathetic condolences from friends and family. It should be a single tear, which slides slowly, with elegance and grace, over a rosy cheek. My sorrow is not elegant. It is black mascara rivers and snot streams. I fear if I let people see the depths of my pain, they would lose trust in the image of the kind and successful woman I have worked so hard to craft. They would judge the negativity which paints my thoughts. They would wonder if I was capable of being a good mother to my children. They would scoff at my professional engagements, declaring "There's no way in hell this woman should be giving advice." My pain is not Disney.

It is "Nightmare on Elm Street". People would gasp and avert their eyes.

And so, I hide. I push all of these fears deep into my soul and lock them away in a dungeon of shame. My outer shell is a better representation of the person I want to be, a shiny exterior painted over a dull and decaying woman. In this way, depression is isolating, like I am an island of pain and despair.

After years of operating in self-imposed emotional isolation, the island is running out of sustenance. If I stay here, I will die here. Alone. I want to connect. I want to reach out. I want to open up. I no longer wish to carry the burden of shame. I need to build a raft.

My raft takes the shape of honest, humble conversation. This candid dialogue begins with my husband. He has stood amongst the carnage of my depression, yet I have never attempted to explain what my depression feels like. I am terrified of his reaction, his judgment, his repulsion. He listens, still and silent. When I am finished, he does not judge. He thanks me for sharing the most vulnerable piece of myself. He *thanks* me.

Despite Miguel's empathy, he does not understand what my depression feels like. And that's okay. How could he possibly understand? It's like people who don't have children. They can imagine the deep levels of love and exhaustion, but they will never truly *understand* until they have children of their own. Miguel's empathy, patience and willingness to listen are enough. Speaking my darkest truth has not driven him away. It has brought us closer.

The next hard conversation I have is with my family doctor, who has known me since I was 10 years old. He is a gentle, caring man who has seen me through broken arms, puberty and childbirth. I trust him because I know he can see me. He can look past my depression and see the woman I want to be, the woman I used to be.

When I share my struggles with him, he provides insight which profoundly changes how I feel about my depression.

"How long have you been feeling this way?" he asks.

"For well over a year and a half," I reply with embarrassment, "I'm not sure why I waited so long to ask for help."

"I know the answer. It's because of pride. You want to be able to fix this yourself and are worried that asking for help makes you weak. You are scared of what others might think," he explains. "Depression is a chemical imbalance in your brain, Kelly. It's not always something you can fix easily or on your own. If you had cancer, you would see a doctor who would prescribe a treatment best suited to your needs. You would reach out to family and friends, who would offer love and support, and care for you in your time of crisis. Depression is also a medical disorder, except people choose to suffer alone. They have a hard time reaching out because they think they should be able to fix themselves."

Part of my shame stems from the idea I *should* be able to help myself. I have built a career and a reputation on my ability to teach people how to cope with intense emotions. I empathetically guide others through complicated emotions, letting them know that all feelings are valuable and I provide strategies for well-being. Why is it that I can use my knowledge to help so many others, yet I cannot help myself? This conundrum is infuriating and humiliating to me. It leaves me feeling like an imposter.

As my doctor speaks, my mind flashes back to an interaction I had with Miguel months before. I was in a season of darkness, alternating between being catatonic and hysterical. I was either curled up in the fetal position, emotionless and numb, or was crying without reason—and without understanding my uncontrollable sadness. Miguel, bless his heart, was nearing the end of his patience.

"Why don't you just try harder?" he asked, with frustration.

His comment smacked me across the face, sending me reeling.

Try harder? How could I possibly try harder? Even in the midst of my despair, I was working my ass off to overcome my depression. If anyone could beat depression, I was determined it would be me. For almost a year, I had been meditating, exercising, going to therapy, reading about depression, listening to uplifting podcasts, journaling, and, and, and ... And still, depression's fingers gripped me in a deadly chokehold, squeezing out what felt like my last breath. Every ounce of energy I had was poured into going through the motions of each day, trying to hold myself together, protecting those I love from my pain and attempting to "cure" my depression.

Try harder?!

My doctor continued, "Having depression is no more your fault than someone who has cancer. No one chooses these things."

Those words illuminated my dark world and shone light upon a new realization dawning on me. The only difference between depression and so many other diseases is shame. Depression is not my fault, yet societal perception causes me to hide my pain and blocks me from reaching out for much-needed support. Cancer is socially acceptable. Depression is not. Cancer survivors are deemed heroic in their tireless efforts to fight and thrive. People with depression are looked at as if they are not trying hard enough to be happy.

What. The. Hell?

I am tired of carrying undeserved and unnecessary shame. Finally setting down this heavy baggage was the first step toward my healing. Without my shame, without my fear, I can move forward with lighter footsteps. Depression is not my fault.

LESSON 3:
YOUR DEPRESSION DOES NOT DEFINE YOU.

"Do your mistakes define you? Do your failures define you? No? Then why would your depression define you? No one is defined by one aspect of their life or their personality. We are beautiful, complicated beings not meant to be shoved in a box and slapped with a label. Don't let one thing become the entirety of who are. You are all the things."

I feared depression was my defining quality, that I *was* a depressed person. It's not true. I refuse to squeeze the wholeness of who I am into that tiny little box. I *have* depression from time to time. It is not *who* I am, but a small facet of my personality.

Yes, I have moments when I struggle with my inner voice. Yes, it affects my relationships, my self-esteem, my parenting, and my ability to deal with stress. I can't deny these things, as much as I wish I could. I wish I didn't have to cope with depression. I wish I didn't have to battle my inner critic, the nasty little asshole who tries to destroy the sense of calm I work so hard to build. I wish I didn't have to work so hard to build my calm! But I do. It's part of who I am. Struggling with my mental health does not make me unlovable. It makes me strong.

I need to find a way to be at peace with this complicated relationship I have with my brain so I can stop despising myself. I wonder if I can find some tiny bit of gratitude, a miniscule sliver of silver lining ...

In those moments in life when I struggle to make sense of my feelings, I often write myself a letter. I offer all of the kindness and advice I would share with a friend who might be in a similar situation. I write with compassion, as if I were talking to my mother, my sister, or a colleague. This practice has usually helped me sort through my thoughts and feelings in a logical and caring way. And so, I challenged myself to write a letter to my depression and find a way to thank it for being a part of me. Even *I* think this approach is cheesy. But, when there's nothing else to lose (except my sanity) ... I'll give it a try.

Dear Depression,

Fuck you.

Try again, Kel. This is not the tone you want to set nor the pathway to peace of mind. In order to release the anger, you need to find acceptance. Start over. Dig deeper.

Dear Depression,

It's true we don't get along. You complicate my life and color my self-concept, but I need to find a way to stop fighting you. It's exhausting and I'm tired of being tired. I hate you because you bring pain to me and those I love. But from the bottom of my heart, I want to investigate other aspects of you. Do you bring any good to my life? How do you serve me? What message am I missing?

Maybe you have made me more empathetic toward the struggles of others. I am a living, breathing example of the anecdote, "You never know what is going on in a person's life." People float in and out of our daily lives, seeming as if they have it all together, but how many people do we truly know? An out-of-character moment, a slip of their guard may hint at a turmoil we rarely see or even know is occurring. I don't judge the person who loses her patience with her children in the grocery store. I don't judge a girlfriend who spends the whole day in bed. I don't judge a colleague who takes a mental health day. We are all doing the very best we can to navigate life's complexities.

Maybe you force me to be vulnerable and to confront my authenticity. Having depression simply doesn't fit with the person I am trying to be. I want to be happy, calm and balanced—or to at least seem that way. However, having my shit together all of the time creates a persona that is unapproachable to others. How can my friends, family, and colleagues be vulnerable with me if I refuse to be vulnerable with them? In the moments when you become a burden too heavy for me to carry alone, I face a choice: let you crush me or ask others to relieve some of the weight. I am learning the power of vulnerability, to let others know when I am not okay. Over and over again, I am surprised at the willingness of others to help and to extend compassion. They don't run from my pain. They aren't disgusted by its ugliness. They are grateful I trust them enough to be real and are proud of my bravery in reaching out.

Maybe you have created a resilience in me that I should be thanking you for. I refuse to give up. This unhappy person is a temporary version of me. It is not who I am at my core. Each day, I choose to rise above, to fight for a better life, for a better version of me. Some days are easier than others, but each day is a choice. I look on the bright side. I get out of bed. I smile at my children. I do something kind for my husband. I do something kind for myself.

I am empathetic. I am authentic. I am vulnerable. I am resilient. I am strong. I am reflective. I am persistent. I am wise. I am a fighter. These are the things that define me. As much as it pains me to admit, I wonder if I would embody these qualities if it weren't for you, Depression. I suppose I should thank you for forcing me to grow. So, thank you. I know it may not be the most heartfelt show of gratitude, but I am working on it.

A half-sincere thank you is better than a hate-filled fuck you. Right?

See? Progress.

Love,

Kel

I AM DEPRESSION

"This is the battleground where you will find out what you are really made of."

1. Are you okay with not being okay?

2. Have you built a support system of friends and family with whom you can be totally vulnerable, and who will walk beside you in your darkest moments? Who are these angels of logic and light in your life?

3. Are there any areas of your life and/or relationships where you can be more authentic?

Chapter 8

THE TRUTH:
"THE ONLY WAY PAST FEAR IS TO WALK THROUGH IT"

There will always be fear. The reason we can't escape fear is simple—the future is unknown. Our world is full of so many what-ifs and uncertainties, things we can't anticipate, tragedies, and adversities. Of course we are afraid! We never know if the next day, the next moment, will deliver us something wonderful or something devastating. It's a challenging way to live, but such is life. This truth is universal, not relegated to a specific few. We all carry this burden, for no one can control the powers of The Universe—though we may try. What we *can* control is our mentality, the mindset with which we view this epic uncertainty.

When I was a young mother, I found myself faced with the first monumental decision I had to make as a parent—to vaccinate or not to vaccinate. You may be thinking, "Sheesh, Kel! The choice seems obvious!" Let me take you back. My indecision occurred in the early 2000s, a time when there was significant conversation linking vaccinations to autism. Current research has evolved, showing no tangible link between the two, however, in those days, a number of people were unsure. That year, when my eldest son was 18 months old, I had two lovely students with autism in my class. Gathering information in an attempt to make an informed decision about vaccinating my child, I chatted with the mothers of my students and asked their opinions on this controversial topic. With so much conflicting research, it seemed beneficial to consult those families who were on the front lines of this adversity and lived with autism as their daily reality. Both mothers did not hesitate before declaring their children were developmentally typical before their 18 month vaccinations. I also asked my doctor, who disagreed resoundingly. There was not enough research to link vaccinations to autism. The developmental onset was purely coincidental.

Confused and under stress, I turned to the only parenting expert I knew at the time, my mother. Thirteen years later, I still remember, verbatim, what she said. "As a mother, you will never be 100% certain of your choices. You will always question yourself. What if you choose to vaccinate your son and he is diagnosed with autism? What if you choose not to, he contracts the measles, becomes sterile and grows up blaming you for your poor decision? You can't play the "What If" Game. If you spend all of your time overthinking the what-ifs, you will become a miserable parent."

I needed to let go of fear, commit to a choice, and have faith everything would work out. It was the first time I realized one of the fundamental truths of adulting—most of the time, we simply cross our fingers and hope for the best.

For more than a decade, I have held this advice close to my heart, not only in regard to my parenting, but also concerning life in general. Fear likes to play the "What If" Game. *What if I don't get that job? What if I fail? What if people judge me?* It's a breeding ground for misery, inadequacy, and self-doubt. *What if* we chose not to play the "What If" Game at all? *What if* we leaned into our fears and rose above our doubts? *What if* we acknowledged our fears and then chose joy instead?

These days, we fear so many things. We often lose sleep over the emotional well-being of our children. We may think we are not enough or not worthy. Sometimes we wonder if we are living our best lives. We might feel a sense of competition with our friends, family and colleagues. There are moments when we panic over our finances and overthink our relationships. We listen to the media and often fret over mass shootings. We watch the news and worry about the racist, sexist and bigoted ideologies people in our society are subjected to. Our brains are so hardwired toward fear, we hardly notice it's there. Instead, we feel pressure, stress, physical pain, and mental illness. We lean away from the discomfort, self-medicating with exercise, food, alcohol and pills—without investigating the root cause of our pain.

I've had enough of being afraid. Haven't you? The steady rise of depression, anxiety, and human disconnection in our society is highly concerning. It's afflicting our children and our elderly. This state of numbness, loneliness, and fear has become an accepted norm. Why isn't there more conversation about this? Why aren't more people standing up and screaming, "What the hell is happening to us?" Instead of asking the obvious questions and doing the hard work, many people keep reaching toward emptiness, searching for fulfillment in all the wrong ways. We might be popping pills (no judgment—I'm included in that category), shopping, drinking, and staying busy when we should be slowing down and engaging in self-reflection. Why is this happening? Why are people so afraid? Why am *I* so afraid?

Writing this book was a catharsis for me, a way to walk toward my fear instead of hiding from it. For years, I had been trying to find a way around my fear. Step over it. Nope. Slide under it. Access denied. Walk around it. Try again, fool. Turn my back and ignore it. That one works for a while, until I realize I will never be able to forge ahead. The only way to work to get past fear is to walk straight into the fire. This book was my attempt to do just that.

At first, airing my fears felt unflattering, shameful. I couldn't believe the extent to which I had let anxiety, worry, and judgment affect me. But as I pressed on, through pain and discomfort, I began to understand the inherent power in the process. As I walked through the fire, I realized I was actually fireproof. My fear only hurt me if I let it. Debunking my inner demons didn't erase my fears, but gave me the strength and wisdom to carry them with more grace.

I am beginning to wonder if it is possible to be rid of fear. Can one truly be fearless? Do I want to be fearless?

The fears I experience seem like a cosmic game of Whack-a-Mole. As soon as I come to terms with one, another pops up behind me. My fears morph and change as life morphs and changes. As my marriage evolves, I am able to let go of some worries, but new ones inevitably arise. As my children grow, I become more comfortable and uncomfortable at the same time. As my career follows a new path, I trust the choice I have made but am nervous about what is to come. It seems that Fear is destined to be my partner in life, my constant companion. Perhaps the goal is not to live a life *without* Fear, but to acknowledge it and learn to sit with it.

I see you, Fear. You can no longer sneak up on me, for I am profoundly aware of your presence. I respect you, for I know that you are here to prepare me for life, loss, adversity and disappointment. I'm learning to be okay with all of that.

I see you, Fear, but I refuse to let you control me. We can sit together, but I will continue to make my own choices. Despite your presence and constant reminders, I will go forth and reach for the life I am meant to live. I want to thrive, Fear, and I won't let you stop me. You don't own me.

How can you take back your power and live a life with less stress, more joy, and greater intention? Well, the good news is, you have already started to do the work by reading this book and completing the journal pages. Virtual high-five to you! I am proud of you and you should be proud of yourself! But what comes after this book? How can we take what we have learned and apply it in our daily lives, grow it in a way that cultivates a content heart rather than a fearful one?

Here's the thing, the solution is really quite simple and it only requires two steps. Are you ready?

Simply listen, and observe. Once you see fear, it loses its power to control you. In all likelihood, your fear will not disappear the moment you see it, however, it will lose the ability to silently manipulate your behavior. So, be on the lookout for the false stories society is telling you. Have an awareness of the propaganda the media feeds you. Examine your past and ask what narratives your family indoctrinates. Keep your eyes peeled for the inaccuracies you hold close to your heart—ones that color your perspective. Search every nook and cranny of your life for fear. It's a sneaky little bastard and will hide behind your core beliefs, masquerading as tradition or success or values. You need to search it out and call it out. *I see you!*

It can be scary to look inwards, to explore what ideologies we are harboring, to examine our family structure, our relationships and our core beliefs. But we need not be afraid of our fears. We need to scrutinize our fears in order to conquer them. It can be unflattering, most definitely uncomfortable, and sometimes, cringe-worthy. There are so many fears I can't believe I carried for so long! They held me down, made me small, and robbed me of my power. I am not that girl any more. I am more intentional, more self-aware, and I walk with more confidence. I feel lighter, freer because I shed an enormous weight when I acknowledged my fear and reclaimed control of my life.

I want the same for you, dear reader. I want you to become empowered and brave. I want you to find your inner warrior and know that she is strong enough to walk through the fire and come out the other side. Your warrior is not afraid of Fear. She nods her head in Fear's direction, then struts toward her own journey, knowing she is destined to fulfill her own potential. Your warrior knows the path will be fraught with challenge, with disappointment, with blood, sweat and tears. She's okay with it. She knows the adversity will be worth the reward.

What the Warrior Says:

FINAL LESSON:
GIRL, YOU'VE GOT THIS!

THE ONLY WAY PAST FEAR IS TO WALK THROUGH IT

"Girl, you've got this!"

1. Take a few minutes to explore the idea of sitting with fear, rather than wishing to become fearless. Which concept rings true for you?

CONCLUSION

I found it fascinating to write this book amid a world health crisis. To witness my country's journey through fear alongside my own emotional journey was riveting. When the virus first broke, half a world away, people watched with interest, remarking on how other countries reacted to a widespread illness. As this crisis crept closer to home, anxiety ramped up and confusion set in. I believe most of us were caught off guard, assuming something like this would never happen in our own backyard. The realization this was happening set off a catalyst of events: school closures, event cancellations, social distancing. Airports closed and hospitals overflowed. The spark of fear was ignited as our community prepared for the worst. A collective shock settled into our bones. To be honest, I wasn't scared of the virus, of becoming ill. What frightened me was the reaction of our society. For a moment, the mentality of some became every man for himself. Global panic was possible because the embers of fear were already burning.

In the first few days of the pandemic, there was a lot to be afraid of as we were encouraged to stay home, isolate, quarantine. *Will people travelling abroad be able to come home? Will people lose their businesses? If we can't work, how will we pay the bills? Will we lose our homes? How will our children remember this stressful and uncertain time? Will it become their childhood trauma?*

The prime minister of Canada addressed the people. This is bad, he said. This is scary. But you are not in this alone. We are in this together. If you are lonely, remember we are all lonely. If you are frightened, take solace in the knowledge we are all frightened. You are not alone. The government is working to protect you and we need to take care of each other. Reach out to your neighbor and see if they have enough to eat. FaceTime with a friend and talk through your worries. Play with your children and remind them they are safe and loved. You are not alone.

It was the voice of reason we all needed to hear and as we settled into a new normal, and I felt a shift in our collective mentality. The posts on social media ceased to be about closures and cancellations, scary statistics, and photos of people in hospital beds. People began to post messages of support and love. There were videos of citizens standing on their balconies, playing instruments to entertain the neighbors and singing the national anthem in solidarity. Friends shared resources about coping with anxiety and tips for how to entertain children at home. People posted inspirational quotes and reminders to stay positive and calm. We applauded our first responders. We recognized the fear and chose to rise above. As the collective fear began to dissipate, it was replaced by the need for human connection.

When fear settles in, fight the urge to regress inwards, to become trapped in the toxicity of your thoughts. If you are anything like me, you may view fear as a weakness and your instinct is to bury it or to hibernate, withdraw. Fight through that urge! When we refuse to vocalize our fears, they grow large and out of control. So, call a friend. Have coffee with a family member. Call a helpline. Talk about your worries because the antidote to fear is human connection.

Read that again. It's vital!

> The antidote to fear is human connection.

It's like we have all been trained, from a very young age, to sit alone in our suffering. One solitary human, stranded and starving on a deserted island. We look around us for food and fresh water, finding none and we marinate in fear, knowing we are going to die. But we stay, close to the place in which we were shipwrecked. It's not comfortable, but it's familiar. However, on the other side of the island, there are people. People who know where the fruit trees are, who know where the freshwater stream bubbles. People who are building a life raft. People who are working together to survive. If only we had the courage to explore, to walk to the other side of the island, we could be saved. We need others. No one can survive alone.

You see, we are a shared humanity in joy and in pain. I guarantee, whatever adversity you currently face, you are not alone. Someone else on this planet is experiencing the same pain or struggle. Maybe they have walked through the fire and can lead you to the other side. Perhaps they are still in the trenches alongside you and can offer empathy and understanding. Whatever your fear, big or small, I urge you to push through the discomfort and reach out.

Sometimes, simply saying something out loud will strip a fear of its power. There are times when I will say to Miguel or to a girlfriend, "I need to tell you my worries. You don't need to respond. You don't need to make them better. I just need to let them go." Other times, I am seeking wisdom, advice or compassion. Knowing someone understands your struggles makes them an easier weight to bear.

For most of my adult life, I have made the mistake of carrying my worries, tucked in my back pocket, ignored and unaddressed. I have plastered on my Game Face and walked into the world with a carefully crafted image of having my shit together. It cost me, big time. It cost me meaningful relationships. It cost me opportunities for connection. It cost me happiness. It cost me my mental health.

The grand misconception of this book may be that I want you to live a life without fear. That's not my intention. Living without fear is impossible. We need fear. The intention of this book is to understand fear and the purpose fear has in our lives. It's when we don't understand fear's function that it begins to take hold of us, with a tight and strangling grip. Fear is a powerful emotion.

It serves as a red flag, signaling an underlying need. The need for safety, the need to belong, the need for acceptance, the need for reassurance. When you feel afraid, dig in, dig deep. What lies beneath the fear? Instead of ignoring the discomfort you feel, what would happen if you walked toward it, investigated your emotions without judgment, and addressed the larger need?

Let's digress for a moment. You may not believe in a larger plan, a force bigger than ourselves and that's okay. I do, however, and I can't help but contemplate the coincidence of me writing this book during such tumultuous times. When I began writing, I was questioning the role fear played in our daily lives, in our relationships, and in our decisions. I saw fear as a negative influence and searched for a way to rid it from my life. Everywhere I looked, I saw fear and I didn't like its prevalence.

I am thankful I was patient enough to let this book take its own journey, for I have not ended where I thought I would. Now, I understand there is value in fear, knowing it is symbolic of our most basic needs. This shift in perspective was a game changer for me. My fear of failure is a need to be accepted for who I am, regardless of my successes. My fear of not being enough is related to my need to belong. Fears about my children and my family structure are tied closely to my need to protect those I love from hurt. My fear of social comparison can be likened to my need to live up to my potential. Once I understood what hid beneath my fear, it became much easier to look at myself with compassion. Fear made me feel weak, but by stepping back and exploring my basic human needs, I was able to see my intentions are noble and I am simply doing the best I can.

I am beginning to wonder if The Universe sent us this virus for a reason, if social distancing may, in fact, be good for us. Let me preface this conversation by stating, in no way am I attempting to negate the colossal economic impact of this health crisis, the mental stress it has caused or the staggering wake of deaths it has left behind. The nature of who I am needs to find a reason for the suffering, a way to learn and grow from the pain. This pondering began when I felt the positive shift in our collective mentality, away from fear and toward connection. It caused me to ask, *what good has come of this? What lessons can be learned from this difficult situation?* Here is what I have concluded:

Mere weeks ago, our society was a fast-paced mecca of social comparison, judgment, pressure to achieve, and superficial connection. It was easy for fear to remain undetected as most of us were simply too busy and too exhausted to notice. In the days since we have been advised to stay home, society's hectic pace has halted to a standstill. People have no choice but to be home with their families. We realize how much we miss our friends and we understand how much we have taken for granted. Going to the grocery store used to be an inconvenience for many of us. Now we are grateful when there is food available on shelves. We would often pass by our neighbors, barely making eye contact, as we rushed to our next appointment. Now, a smile and a wave are gestures of connection we long for. We take pleasure in the small things—a sunny day, our children's laughter, a chat with a friend. We have created a feeling of community support, shop at the local store, take care of others, do the right thing for the greater good. We walked through the initial fear of this situation and were able to re-evaluate our priorities. It's no longer every man for himself. The collective mentality has become *we* before me.

I am left with this question, what becomes of us once this crisis is over? How will we take forward the lessons learned to become better people, a better society? I like to believe that once we recognize fear, it's difficult to un-see. We can't ignore fear any longer. It has been shoved in our faces and revealed unflattering sides of our society. Now that we have seen fear rear its ugly head, what are we going to do with it? In recent weeks, our society has grown, shown empathy, and reached out to connect on an emotional level. Can we carry this feeling of shared humanity into our everyday lives, once the regular pace resumes?

Maybe I am being naïve. As much as I would like to control the fate of our society, Miguel tells me I cannot. I can only focus on me and work to control the extent to which fear influences my life. I can also hope you will focus on your own growth. Now that you have investigated your own fears, what will you do with this information? Don't let all of this work be in vain. If we all continue to do the work, to expand our self-awareness, to be cognizant of our fears, and to walk through the fire toward personal growth, I believe a societal shift on a permanent level is possible.

When we acknowledge fear, stare it straight in the eyes and choose to move forward, anything becomes possible. Stand strong in the rocky season of your relationship! Allow your children room to make mistakes! Chase your dreams and create space for your own failures! Ask that girl to dance! Reach for his hand, even when it means being vulnerable!

At the beginning of this book, I asked you to imagine a life without fear. Scrap that ridiculous idea. We were so sweet and innocent then, weren't we? The wiser version of me now proposes the following thought. I hope you take time to ponder the meaning and depth of it. Don't rush your response. Sit with it. Mull it over. Truly give it the wondering it deserves. It's a simple thought, but holds, within it, the potential to alter your course.

What would your life look like, if you refused to let Fear keep you small?

EPILOGUE

The Warrior grabs my left arm and holds it up for me to see. We both stare at the tattooed letters which encircle my wrist.

"Do you understand that the goal is not to be fearless?" she asks.

"Yes," I answer. "If you think you can escape fear, you are fooling yourself. Fear is ever-present, and has the potential to hold us back, but fear can also serve us. Fear is a warning, an inkling, a sign something isn't right. Fear can drive us toward change, and prepare us for hard things. Fear prompts us to question, to examine, and prevents us from walking through life on autopilot. Just as there is no resilience without challenge, there is no courage without fear. Instead of pretending I am fearless, I need to own my fear, recognize it and listen to what it's telling me. I guess I need to make friends with fear."

"You don't need to make friends with fear," scoffed The Warrior. "You need to make Fear your bitch!"

ACKNOWLEDGMENTS

To Mickey, mi rey y mi amor. Thank you for being my rock and my foundation. Thank you for loving me even when I couldn't love myself. Thank you for your patience when I disappear into my writing, lost in my own thoughts and for being there when I emerge once again.

To my mama, who is always the first person to read my work. Thank you for your open-mindedness, for reading without ego or judgment, even when it hurts. Thank you for understanding that I am not asking permission, but am sharing a piece of myself. Your unwavering love and support inspires me to be a better mother and a better human.

To Ray, who has read my stories since I was a little girl. Thank you for sharing a love of words, for offering your honest feedback and for taking the time to make me a better writer.

To Krista and Ashley. I can't thank you enough for believing in me, for championing me and for being excited about my work. Because of your strong, passionate leadership and encouragement, I am living my dream of being a writer. You helped change my course and I will be forever grateful.

To the two young men who will eternally be my babies. Thank you for loving me and forgiving me over and over, even when I didn't deserve it. You are my purpose.

About the Author

While Kelly may seem like a hot mess and most days she is okay with that, professionally, she's got it all together! Kelly works as a writer, speaker, and educator. She currently teaches at the University of British Columbia and acts as a consultant for the Dalai Lama Center for Peace and Education. She is also a freelance writer for Merack Publishing and Island Parent magazine.

Kelly lives with her husband and children in a wonderful little bubble she has created half-way between her ex-husband's residence and her parents' house. (Residing comfortably close to both, but not too close.) She is incredibly grateful to live in Vancouver, British Columbia, finding endless joy from the beauty of the local mountains and the mystifying power of the ocean.

When she's not working, Kelly enjoys nature (cliché!), painting (calming!), exercise (necessary!) and making cheesy music videos with her family (the most fun ever!)

You should absolutely read other work written by Kelly: *Raising Resilient Children* and *Ridiculous, Resilient Me.*

Check out her website www.kellycleeve.com and join her Facebook group on women's empowerment: Radiant and Resilient or on parenting: Raising Resilient Children

Manufactured by Amazon.ca
Bolton, ON

14173076R00113